W0011024

The
National Parks
and Other Wild Places of
Australia

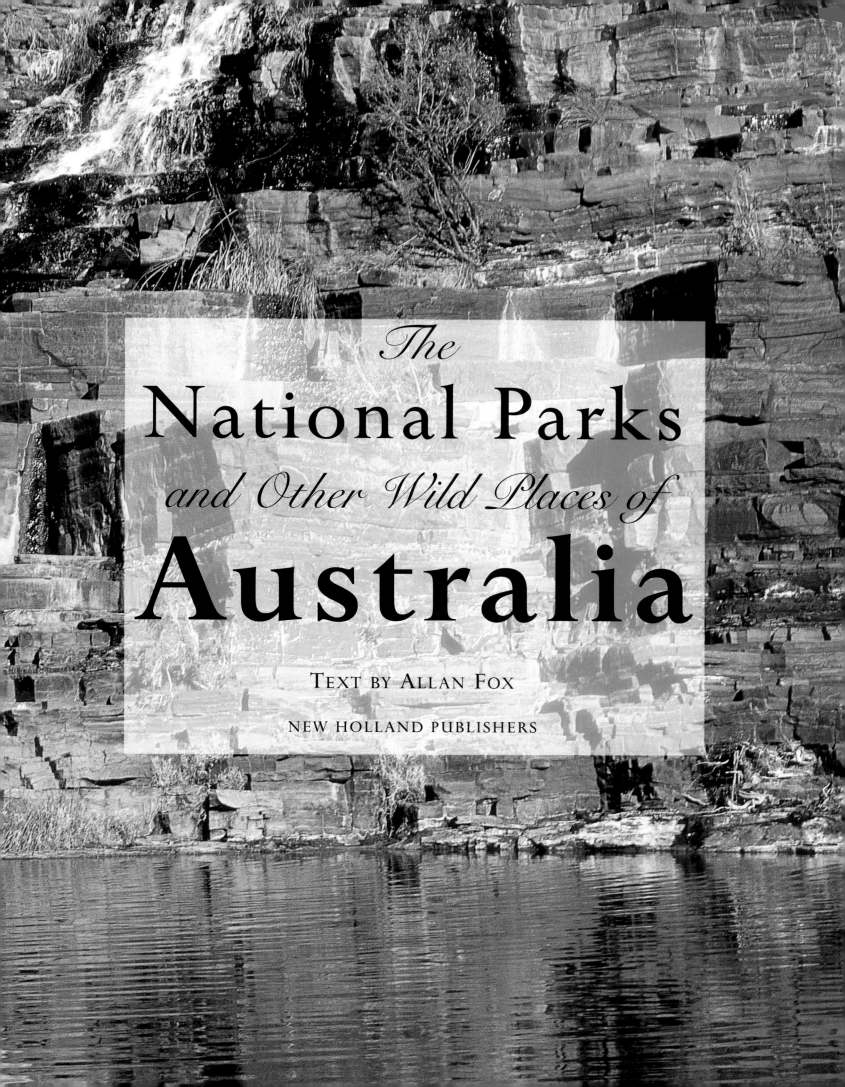

The
National Parks
and Other Wild Places of
Australia

Text by Allan Fox

NEW HOLLAND PUBLISHERS

First published in the UK in 2000 by New Holland Publishers (UK) Ltd
London • Cape Town • Sydney • Auckland

24 Nutford Place, London W1H 6DQ, United Kingdom
80 McKenzie Street, Cape Town 8001, South Africa
14 Aquatic Drive, Frenchs Forest NSW 2086, Australia
218 Lake Road, Northcote Auckland, New Zealand

1 3 5 7 9 10 8 6 4 2

ISBN 1 85974 609 8

Publishing General Manager: Jane Hazell
Publisher: Averill Chase
Publishing Manager: Anouska Good
Project Editor: Kathy Metcalfe
Editor: Emma Wise

Designer: Peter Bosman
Cartography: Carl Germishuys
Picture Controller: Kirsti Wright
Reproduction by: PICA Colour Separation
Printed by: Star Standard Industries Pte Ltd

PUBLISHERS' NOTE

Throughout this book species are, where possible, referred to by their common as opposed to scientific names for ease of reference by the reader. Where no common names exist, scientific names are used. The maps contained in the book are intended as 'locators' only; detailed, large-scale maps should be consulted when planning a trip. It is important to note that access, accommodation and other details vary as new transport methods and facilities develop. Remember that trail routes and weather conditions can vary, so always plan ahead. Inform the local authorities of your travel plans when you arrive and ask park rangers about local conditions and wildlife to ensure your visit is a safe one. Although the publishers have made every effort to ensure that the information contained in this book was correct at the time of going to press, they accecpt no responsibility for any loss, injury or inconvenience sustained by any person using this book

MAP LEGEND FOR PARK MAPS			
Main road		**Brisbane** ◎	City or major town
Secondary road		Daintree ◎	Village or small town
Track		Park HQ ▣	General information
Walking track		*Lookout* ●	Place of interest
Railway		*Murray* R.	Water feature
State boundary		*Mt Kosciuszko* ▲	Peak
Park boundary		Connellan Airport ✈	Airport
Marine park		To Alice Springs →	Directional

P1: *Sunrise from the Viking, Alpine National Park, Victoria.*

PP2–3: *Fortescue Falls, Karijini National Park, Western Australia.*

Opposite: *Mts Gower and Lidgbird across the lagoon from Signal Point,
Lord Howe Island, New South Wales.*

P7: *Grasstrees at sunset across heathlands,
Kalbarri National Park, Western Australia.*

CONTENTS

FOREWORD

Australia's national parks are the icons of the nation's environment. They include the distinctive plants, animals, landscapes and cultural sites that make Australia unique. National parks will only be there for future generations to appreciate and enjoy if this generation looks after this priceless legacy. Ignorance is the greatest threat to the park system. Once people are aware of these areas then the commitment to protect them becomes second nature.

The Australian Heritage Commission (AHC) is a Federal body whose major task is the compilation and maintenance of the Register of the National Estate, which includes both the natural and cultural heritage. This requires extensive and intensive research to classify the national significance of individual areas, historic locations and places. Its work on determining the status and location of Australian wilderness, for example, has been ground-breaking and of the highest quality, which utilised a number of specialised consultants. Much of the Commission's work involves co-operative programmes with the National Trust movement, Nature Conservation Councils and other conservation bodies.

Quality publications such as this book, *National Parks of Australia*, are vital tools that inform society of the values preserved in our national park system. I commend this book to not only those who are committed to the protection of Australia's parks but to those who are embarking on a journey of discovery about the wonders of Australia's environment.

Bruce Leaver
Executive Director, Australian Heritage Commission

PREFACE

Such a work as this is the result of a steady growth of experience over many years in many places and with many people. Being a teacher's son there were always long school holidays and a family who loved travel and the music of the landscape. The urge to travel has never left me; that motivation to discover, to study and to understand our land must be acknowledged. My later guide and mentor who picked me up in teachers' college and lured me late into the New South Wales Wildlife Service and on into the State and Federal Parks and Wildlife Services, was one of Australia's greatest naturalist and environmental teachers, the late Allen Strom. This same travel bug for work and pleasure also left my long suffering family without a father and husband for long portions of each year.

My professional life brought me into contact with many like-minded colleagues and organisations in Australia and overseas, to whom I owe the greatest of gratitude for sharing their inspiration, ideas and knowledge. I particularly wish to express my indebtedness to the following people and organisations. New South Wales: National Parks and Wildlife Service and its past and present staff, particularly the late Don Johnstone, Alastair Howard, Roger Good, Alan Morris, Charles Boyd, the late Fred Hersey, David Hope, Wendy Goldstein, Sharyn Sullivan and Chris O'Brien. Northern Territory: Conservation Commission, later called the Parks and Wildlife Commission, past and present staff, particularly Derrick Roff, Ian and Paul Cawood, Dr Ken Johnson, Peter King and Marcus Sandford. Queensland: National Parks and Wildlife Service, past and present staff, particularly John Day and Margot Warnett. South Australia: National Parks and Wildlife Service, past and present staff, particularly Nicholas Newland, Robin Young and Neville Gare. Tasmania: National Parks and Wildlife Service, past and present staff. Western Australia: Conservation and Land Management, past and present staff, particularly Dr Andrew Burbidge. Victoria: Parks Victoria, past and present staff, particularly Don Sinclair. Commonwealth: Environment Australia, past and present staff, particularly Ian Morris, Greg Miles, Louis Beens, Anne Jelinek, Peter Wellings, Big Bill Neidgie, Bruce Leaver and our band of Aboriginal ranger trainees, now rangers at Kakadu.

My work also brought me into contact with many academic institutions and the Commonwealth Scientific and Industrial Research Organisation (CSIRO) Divisions and many people in those places gave valuable time, information and inspiration. Dr John Harris, Dr Len Webb, Dr Alec Costin, Dr Harry Recher, Dr Alan Newsome and many others contributed towards moving my mind forward. Much wisdom also resides in non-governmental organisations, who always tested my environmental and resource-use ideas and decisions. My sincere thanks also goes to their memberships for innumerable discussions by the campfire and over a beer.

The structuring of the words and pictures in this book comes from people and places and lends truth to the ethic: 'What is the value of knowledge if it is not shared'. There are still more than 500 Australian national parks not mentioned in this book, so there is much more to share.

Allan Fox
Environmental Management Consultant

Right: *Dawn light over the Serra Range, Grampians National Park, Victoria.*

INTRODUCTION

The vast island continent of Australia is a land of boundless space – of ancient mountain ranges and endless plains, brilliant red deserts, azure seas and the splendour of southern starlit nights. Lying below South-East Asia, between the Indian Ocean and the Pacific, it is the lowest, flattest and, apart from Antarctica, the driest landmass on Earth. Combine these characteristics with an area of over 7.5 million square kilometres (2.9 million square miles) and the result is a place of incredible natural diversity, where a seemingly infinite variety of flora and fauna have adapted in countless ways to their particular habitats.

Towering eucalypts and lush green rainforests vie for the visitor's attention along with surreal rock formations, and plants and animals that are found nowhere else in the world. Australia's unique marsupials include the shy Koala – confined to areas supporting the particular eucalypts they feed upon – and 43 species of the kangaroo and wallaby group, with habitats ranging from the desert to the tropics. Other mammals, birds, amphibians, reptiles, fish and a bewildering assortment of invertebrates are found throughout the land. Along the 36,735 kilometres (22,812 miles) of coast, peerless golden beaches slip into oceans teeming with activity. Tropical seas to the north shelter the largest coral reef system in the world, while the powerful southern waters carve spectacular formations from the often rocky shores.

Nearly one million square kilometres (386,000 square miles) of Australia, 12.8 per cent, is protected in terrestrial and marine national parks and equivalent reserves. Many of these protected areas are in near-wilderness condition, allowing visitors to experience the thrill of exploration. Stretching as it does from the tropics to the Southern Ocean, Australia is also an excellent year-round destination – it is always the perfect time of year somewhere in this vast country.

Opposite: *Snorkellers spend a sublime day exploring Hardy Reef in the warm tropical waters of Queensland's Great Barrier Reef Marine Park.*

Above: *From late winter flowering wattles light up the Australian bush in colours ranging from bright golden yellow to the palest of creams.*

A Long Human History

Australia's diverse cultural mix is a product of exploration, transportation, immigration and over 60,000 years of habitation. Before European settlement began with the first transportation of convicts in 1788, Australia was occupied by 250 or so different language groups of Aboriginal people with a continuous culture running back at least 62,000 years. This culture, which places the people within the landscape instead of apart from it, is richly described in art, dance and story.

Contemporary Australia has its origins as a British colony, with influxes of migrants from all over the world, particularly from Europe and Asia. Current moves towards a reconciliation between the traditional owners of the land and Australians who trace their ancestry back to cultures overseas have resulted in the handback and Aboriginal co-management of a number of national parks (*see below*).

An Island Commonwealth

Australia is comprised of six States and two mainland Territories, most of which have extensive coastlines and encompass enormous expanses of land. Borders tend to run along rivers or lines of latitude and longitude. Until 1901, the six States were six independent colonies, each with colonial capitals, loosely cooperating under the British flag. On 1 January 1901, after much consultation and debate, the six colonies federated to form the Commonwealth of Australia.

Today's five mainland States are New South Wales, Victoria, Queensland, South Australia and Western Australia. The island State of Tasmania, south of Victoria, is separated from the mainland by Bass Strait, 220 kilometres (137 miles) in width. The two Territories are the Australian Capital Territory – surrounding the country's planned capital Canberra and including Jervis Bay, Canberra's 'port' near Sydney – and the Northern Territory. Each State and Territory, apart from the ACT, also has its own coastal capital city. Sydney, the capital of New South Wales, and Melbourne, the capital of Victoria, are the largest.

The vast majority of Australians today live on or near the coast, with a high percentage living in and around the capital cities. Over 85 per

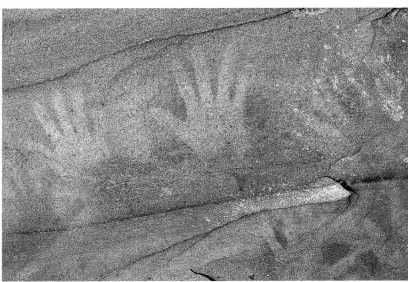

cent of the population is concentrated in the south-eastern corner of the country and, consequently, much of rural and outback Australia is very thinly populated with vast areas completely unoccupied.

Breaking Away from Gondwana

Extending from the mid-tropics just south of the equator to deep into the cool temperate zone, this southern continent has always been isolated from Asia by an oceanic barrier of at least 70 kilometres (43.5 miles), even during the periods of lowest sea-level.

For over 50 million years after breaking clear from the ancient southern super-continent Gondwana, this vast continental plate populated by Gondwanan plant and animal systems has rafted northwards towards the equator. Its living cargo has been the source from which much of Australia's native flora and fauna has evolved.

As the continent drifted north away from the remains of Gondwana, it entered drier latitudes. The temperate rainforest habitats covering much of Australia, rich in species, came under stress. Eucalypts adapted well to the drier conditions producing today's 550 species, most occurring in woodland and tall open forest formations. One group of eucalypt species – the low, multi-stemmed mallee – favoured arid areas, other eucalypts the tropics, while grand old River Red Gums sank their roots deep into the sands of riverbeds in arid regions.

Three million years ago, Australia drifted close enough to Indonesia for some bird species as well as rodents, bats and many plant species to migrate to these shores. Further speciation was stimulated by the ice ages of the past 100,000 years. Today, Australia's 25,000 plant species – almost all of which are evergreen – illustrate effective adaptations to fires, droughts and the ancient phosphate-deficient soils.

Above left: A carpet of wildflowers covers the red earth in the Kennedy Range National Park at the arid edge of the Pilbara in Western Australia.

Above right: Aboriginal hand stencils cover the walls of Red Hand Cave in the Blue Mountains National Park behind Sydney in New South Wales.

Red Heart, Living Green

Today, pictures of Australia from space show a vast island continent with a shimmering reddish yellow heart surrounded by layers of ever-increasing green. A long blue-green strip, the well-worn Great Dividing Range, runs down the length of the east coast, purple ranges and plateaux slashed by giant gorges rise off the centre and the west, while ancient meandering streams of white sand drain into a central blistered set of gleaming salt lakes as large as small seas.

Across the north, the shining Coral, Arafura and Timor seas lap lonely coasts where tropical wet season floods sweep through bands of bright green mangroves. But the greenest of greens are reserved for the pockets of rainforest and the island State of Tasmania.

Rainforests, wet and dry eucalypt forests, woodlands, scrublands, alpine meadows, grasslands, heathlands, shrublands and deserts are just some of the habitats harbouring kangaroos, koalas, wombats, possums, and many other marsupials, including the unusual egg-laying mammals or monotremes – the Platypus and the echidna. There are also 756 bird species, many with brilliant plumage, and somewhere between two and three hundred thousand kinds of animals.

Nature Conservation Begins

The Aboriginal people of Australia believe that through their great creation ancestors they have a connection with everything that is natural. They see themselves as part of the place and its living fabric, and they see the place as part of themselves. Use of fire for hunting, for 'cleaning' the land, gradually changed habitat in some places and, over the thousands of generations of human presence, plant and animal populations evolved in response to the fire and hunting regimes.

In addition, the incredible complexity of Aboriginal socio-religious and kinship systems, all of which are intimately connected with the land, maintained very significant protected areas for many important totemic species. From 1788, when Sydney became the first European settlement, concentrations of humans with little understanding of the Australian landscape began to place increasing demands upon fixed

areas of land. Judge Barron Field of the Supreme Court of New South Wales stated: 'no tree to my taste can be beautiful that is not deciduous ... it is not of us, and it is nothing to us'. However, even as early as 1802–3, just 14 years after settlement, the Governor of New South Wales was forced to establish controls on tree felling and taking cedar.

The First 'National Park' in the World

The 19th century saw a general growth in interest in the natural sciences, highlighting the scientific value of the Australian landscape and its flora and fauna. Art and literature blossomed, defining the grandeur of the rugged ranges and sweeping plains, and the unique plants and animals of this brilliant sunlit country. By the 1850s politicians began to be drawn to the idea that some lands needed to be protected. Each of the States, beginning with Tasmania in 1863, began to enact laws to protect areas of special environmental significance and, in so doing, established the conflict that continues today between protection and exploitation of the environment.

Colonial Secretary and Minister for Lands, Sir John Robertson, and many others living in Sydney, became alarmed by outbreaks of smallpox and plague, and the deterioration of the health of the urban people. Robertson began a campaign assisted by prominent citizens to reserve a place that could be 'lungs for Sydney'. That place, on the southern fringes of the city, was proclaimed The National Park in 1879 – Australia's first national park and the first time this designation for land had been used in law anywhere in the world.

A Citizen's Movement

Although Tasmania and Queensland set up rudimentary management agencies for national parks, the other State systems would not have been at all effective without the continued leadership and support of the public and of a number of learned societies.

These societies were joined by popular field naturalist clubs in pressuring government for park establishment and becoming active in protected area management. In New South Wales the first of the

protection-oriented activist societies, The Wildlife Preservation Society of Australia, was formed by Dr David Stead in 1909. That State also benefited from the small but highly effective National Parks and Primitive Area Council led by the 'father of wilderness' in Australia, Myles Dunphy. These were later joined by the National Trusts, National Parks Associations and the Australian Conservation Foundation.

In 1948, the Fauna Protection Act in New South Wales triggered a series of changes in Australia's political climate that eventually led to that state passing the country's first National Parks and Wildlife Act in 1967. Other States and Territories soon followed suit.

Diverse Protection

Generally speaking, the State and Territory governments have jurisdiction over the lands within their borders. This means that apart from two national parks – Uluru–Kata Tjuta and Kakadu in the Northern Territory – and seven areas on external Territories, the national park and protected area systems have been established and are managed by the various State and Territory governments. It was not until 1972 that these governments, through the Council of Nature Conservation Ministers (CONCOM), managed to reach agreement on the following definition for an Australian National Park:

> A National Park is a relatively large area set aside for its features of predominantly unspoiled natural landscape, flora and fauna, permanently dedicated for public enjoyment, education and inspiration, and protected from all interference other than essential management practices, so that its natural attributes are preserved.

Above left: *The Rick Rack Banksia,* Banksia speciosa, *is one of hundreds of plant species in the Fitzgerald River National Park in Western Australia.*

Above right: *The fluted rock walls of Kantju Gorge in the Uluru–Kata Tjuta National Park in the Northern Territory glow deep red at sunset.*

Such a diversity of establishment authority has led to no less than 47 different kinds of protected areas in Australia. The reasons for reservation are incredibly varied and range from the sustainable management of particular species, ecosystems, landscapes and historic areas to the protection of specific features such as geological units, shipwrecks or particular environmental education areas.

As well as more than 520 national parks – ranging in size from tiny coral cays to the immense Kakadu National Park, 19,804 square kilometres (7,644 square miles) in area – there are over 5,250 other reserved areas. Over 3,100 of these are strict non-recreational nature reserves or their equivalents, many larger and more significant than some of the national parks and often inaccessible. Some of these are also World Biosphere Reserves and considered to be of supreme scientific value. Others have become crucial baseline environmental areas because of the accumulated knowledge from numerous long-term research programs. Australia now has 12 World Biosphere Reserves and 12 areas with World Heritage listing. With so many special places to choose from, this book focuses on important reserves that also fall within the traditional concept of a national park.

Conservation Today

Australia today is evolving novel approaches to the conservation management of some large areas of sensitive environment to ensure the sustainability of the natural systems. Monitoring of ecosystem conditions and management success depends upon both ground surveys and the extensive use of remote sensing and satellite photography. The vast Great Barrier Reef Marine Park, for example, operates under a management system of designated zones ranging from areas of sustainable resource exploitation and tourism to strict nature reserves and national parks.

The scientific managers of park ecosystems have also come to realise that managing national parks sustainably demands a dynamic mix of long-term experience and occupational knowledge with present-day science. Kakadu, Uluru–Kata Tjuta, Gurig, Nitmiluk and Watarrka national parks of the Northern Territory and, most recently, Mutawintji in New South Wales have now been returned to the traditional owners and are jointly managed by those owners and by the relevant government park services. The traditional owners live modified traditional lives within the Northern Territory parks.

Other national park areas, such as the Gammon Ranges in South Australia and Millstream-Chichester in Western Australia, have management structures that work closely with the indigenous people. To have an Aboriginal interpreter describe and explain the significance and traditional stories of a place is fascinating as well as a great privilege. For example, such is the depth of cultural memory that local coastal people still refer accurately to the geography of the land beneath the Arafura Sea as their ancestors experienced it before the sea reached its present level 6,000 years ago.

In most national parks some very special sites of sacred significance are only accessible to specific traditional owners. Visitors should always respect the local people's cultural life as well as their privacy – park signs will usually indicate appropriate behaviour. Photography of the people by strangers is generally out of the question.

Visiting Australia's Protected Areas

Management of Australian national parks has followed the North American model, providing ranger services, visitor information centres and interpretive services as well as track systems offering a range of options from short self-guided nature walks to multi-day wilderness walks, camping and caravan sites with varied facilities and, in major tourist areas, concessions for the development and management of resorts and accommodation. When planning a visit, it is important first to contact the relevant authority for advice (see page 174), as bookings

and other special circumstances may apply. Visitors should also remember that all native flora and fauna in all Australian national parks is protected and should not be removed or interfered with in any way.

This book includes visitor information panels for each park described – these include the park's general location and climate, the best time of year to visit, access, permits required, facilities available, wildlife-spotting opportunities and suggestions for possible activities and what to bring. Because Australia's climate ranges from alpine to desert to wet tropical, with many variations in between, visitors should be careful when planning what clothing and footwear to take.

Taking Care in the Bush

Australia's many venomous snakes and spiders are rarely seen and, while a small number can be deadly, they do not pose a major threat. Snakes are most lively in the warmer months from September to April, although they may be seen at any time in the coastal tropics and they like to wander about the desert on summer evenings.

Mosquito-borne diseases such as Ross River Fever pose a bigger problem, so use an insect repellent in areas prone to mosquitoes, particularly in the evening and early mornings. The Box Jellyfish or Marine Stinger has claimed 80 lives since 1880 – children are particularly at risk – so try to avoid swimming in shallow near-shore tropical waters from Broome in Western Australia across the north to Bundaberg in Queensland from October to May. Use vinegar to wash off any tentacles sticking to the skin, do not use alcohol of any kind.

To avoid heatstroke in the high temperatures of the outback between October and March, wear a broad-brimmed hat, light clothing over most of the body and drink at least a litre of water every two hours. Most importantly, if your vehicle breaks down on a desert road, do not leave it. High ultraviolet levels mean visitors should use sunscreen – SPF 30+ in alpine areas, deserts, at the seaside and in the tropics.

Wildlife Watching and Botanizing

Apart from the birds, most Australian wildlife is nocturnal and cryptic, and none of the furred animals in the wild pose a threat to people. Sightings will usually be the result of chance encounters, so it is wise to visit one of Australia's many fine zoological parks to understand something about your prospective photographic subjects.

The Tidbinbilla Nature Reserve near Canberra, the Desert Park and Botanic Garden in Alice Springs, the Wildlife Park in Darwin and the Healesville Sanctuary in Melbourne offer the best natural settings and fine interpretation. For marine life, the Great Barrier Reef Marine Park Authority's Aquarium at Townsville is Australia's best coral environment display and other capital city aquaria are all excellent. Sydney and Melbourne zoos provide an excellent general wildlife cover.

For an understanding of Australian native plants, the Canberra National Botanic Gardens are second to none. For desert plants visit Alice Springs' Desert Park and Botanic Gardens and for the incredible West Australian flora, Kings Park in Perth is perfect.

Touchstones of the Wild

Australia's national parks are the touchstones of a once wild continent. Only by experiencing them for yourself will you begin to know the country. Make sure you tread lightly on the land for when we damage our wild places, we damage the hidden wild places in ourselves.

Opposite far left: *Common Walleroo, Flinders Ranges NP, South Australia.*

Below left: *Crested and Bridled Terns wheel around a sand spit on North Brook Island in the Great Barrier Reef Marine Park, Queensland.*

Below: *An Emu chick feeds with its family in the Brachina Gorge, Flinders Ranges National Park. Chicks lose their distinctive stripes as they mature.*

The **AUSTRALIAN CONTINENT**

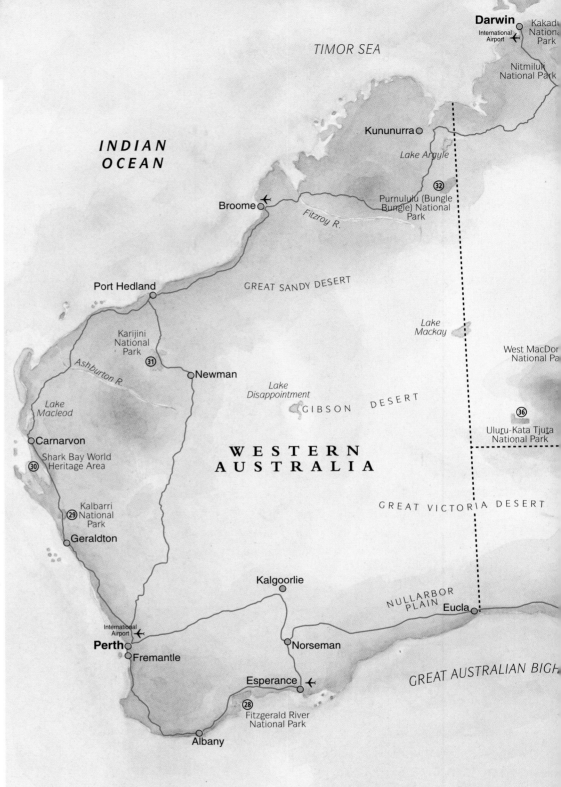

TORRES STRAIT

ARAFURA SEA

GULF OF CARPENTARIA

Weipa

Great Barrier Reef

CORAL SEA

Mitchell R.

Daintree National Park
①
Port Douglas
International Airport ✈ Cairns

② Lawn Hill National Park

③ The Great Barrier Reef Marine Park

Tennant Creek

Mount Isa ✈

Townsville ✈

Great Barrier Reef

NORTHERN ERRITORY

ice Springs

QUEENSLAND

SOUTH PACIFIC OCEAN

SIMPSON DESERT

Longreach

Rockhampton

GREAT DIVIDING RANGE

④ Carnarvon National Park

⑤ Fraser Island World Heritage Area

② Witjira National Park

Goyder Lagoon

Lake Eyre

SOUTH AUSTRALIA

Lake Torrens

Gammon Ranges National Park ②

Lake Frome

International Airport ✈ Brisbane
⑥ Lamington National Park

GREAT DIVIDING RANGE

⑦ Dorrigo National Park

Port Augusta

Flinders Ranges National Park ②

Broken Hill

Darling R.

NEW SOUTH WALES

Dubbo

Blue Mountains National Park

⑩ Myall Lakes National Park

Lord Howe Island World Heritage Area

⑧

ort Lincoln

Mungo National Park ⑨

Murrumbidgee R.

Newcastle ⑩
International Airport ✈
⑪
Sydney

International Airport ✈ Adelaide

Murray R.

Royal National Park ⑫

Flinders Chase National Park ㉔

Grampians National Park
⑱ International Airport ✈
Alpine National Park ⑭

VICTORIA

International Airport ✈

Canberra
ACT

⑬ Kosciuszko National Park

⑮

Croajingolong National Park

TASMAN SEA

Port Campbell National Park ⑰

Melbourne

Wilsons Promontory National Park ⑯

BASS STRAIT

Cradle Mountain-Lake St Clair National Park

Launceston

Mount Field National Park
㉓ International Airport ✈
㉒ ㉑
Franklin-Gordon Wild Rivers National Park
⑳ Hobart

Freycinet National Park ⑲

Southwest National Park

TASMANIA

N

AUSTRALIA

THAILAND LAOS
Bangkok VIETNAM
CAMBODIA Ho Chi Minh City

Manila
PHILIPPINES

SOUTH CHINA SEA

PACIFIC OCEAN

Kuala Lumpur MALAYSIA
SINGAPORE Pontianak

Equator

Jakarta INDONESIA Ujung Pandang

PAPUA NEW GUINEA

NEW BRITAIN

SOLOMON ISLANDS

MELANESIA

Kupang

INDIAN OCEAN

Darwin

Port Moresby

Cairns

CORAL SEA

NEW CALEDONIA Noumea

AUSTRALIA

Tropic of Capricorn

Brisbane

Perth

Adelaide Canberra Sydney
Melbourne

SOUTHERN OCEAN

TASMANIA Hobart

NEW ZEALAND

Auckland

NORTH ISLAND

SOUTH ISLAND

KEY

———	Main road
- - - -	State boundary
Sydney ○	City
Cairns ○	Town
Murray	Water feature
✈	Airport

AUSTRALIA

0 _____ 250 _____ 500 km

0 _____ 125 _____ 250 miles

QUEENSLAND

Queensland is the second largest of Australia's eight States and Territories, with a land area of 1,733,000 square kilometres (668,938 square miles). Occupying the north-eastern quarter of the continent, the State spreads across a range of climatic zones, from the Torres Strait and the Gulf of Carpentaria in the tropical north to the temperate south and the vast arid inland.

The coastline, including islands, extends for 9,800 kilometres (6,086 miles). Much of it is protected by the spectacular Great Barrier Reef – the most extensive sequence of coral reefs in the world and the backbone of the vast Great Barrier Reef Marine Park. South of the reef, along the Great Sandy coast, the Fraser Island World Heritage Area shelters the largest sand island in the world.

The Great Dividing Range follows the Pacific coast of Australia from the tip of Cape York down through Queensland's Central Highlands, on through New South Wales and the Australian Capital Territory to Victoria in the south. In the heart of the Queensland highlands, the white canyons of Carnarvon Gorge National Park contain magnificent 'galleries' of Aboriginal rock art. The great divide separates Queensland's forested east from the grass and savanna country to the west, which in turn, gives way to the flat south-western Channel Country and the desert. Queensland's longest rivers – the Georgina, Diamantina and the Thompson (which becomes Cooper Creek) – spread during flood into hundreds of channels and billabongs across the vast plains of the usually dry south-west. Far to the north, six major rivers flow into the Gulf of Carpentaria. The relatively quiet waters of this vast gulf are lined with mangrove forests, as is most of Australia's tropical coast.

Rising in the ranges as the majority of east coast rivers do, the wild and raging Barron, Mulgrave, Tully and Herbert rivers crash down gorges from the high peaks behind Cairns. Here, the highest rainfall in Australia supports thousands of square kilometres of tropical rainforests and tall eucalypt forests. North of Cairns, the core of the wet tropics is the Daintree National Park – 'where the rainforest meets the reef' – the perfect introduction to tropical Queensland.

DAINTREE NATIONAL PARK

Heart of the Wet Tropics

The 500 kilometres (311 miles) between Townsville and Cooktown in northern Queensland is a region of spectacular forested mountain ranges. A steep staircase of five rainforest types drops from the mist forests of the mountain tops down to the wet tropical rainforest by the gleaming waters of the Coral Sea.

Established in 1967, the 760 square kilometres (293 square miles) of Daintree National Park, is the core of the State's wet tropics. It is one of 19 national parks that form part of the Wet Tropics of Queensland World Heritage Area, where Mount Bartle Frere, the State's highest mountain, receives up to a staggering 10,000 millimetres (394 inches) of rain per year.

Isolated from species evolving in other lands, the largest concentrations of primitive living flowering plants anywhere in the world survive uncontaminated in pockets of Queensland's wet-tropic rainforests. The Daintree National Park, including the Cape Tribulation section north of Cairns, is famous for its enchanting stands of Native Fan Palms and unusual animals, such as the Daintree Ringtail Possum and the Green Python. World Heritage listing of this area of Queensland's wet tropics in 1988 shut down most of the regional rainforest timber industry, which received millions of dollars in compensation from the Australian government.

Variety, the Spice of Rainforest Life

The variety of species in the Daintree rainforests is astounding. Without even stepping from a car parked in the trackhead carpark at Mossman Gorge, at least 20 different plant families can be seen in the trees alone, including the olive, lychee, mango, avocado, lemon, fig and guava. Then there is Nutmeg, a Flame Tree, bean, palm and Star Apple as well as poinsettia, Silky Oak, Blueberry Ash and Red Cedar. Over 1,000 tree species in the wet tropic forests represent these and other families. The forest floor and the trees themselves carry probably another 2,000 species of plants.

An isolated Stonewood Tree on the forest edge – called *Mukurun* by the Yuku Yalanji Aboriginal people and *Backhousia hughesii* by scientists – has very hard wood and even harder gum, which sets like stone and was used by the Yuku Yalanji people as a cement. Identified by a pale greyish, flaky bark, the tree bears masses of small creamy white blossoms on thin stalks.

Growing on this tree are at least three epiphytic fern species and four species of semi-epiphytes, as well as an umbrella fern, a *Fragraea* and two fig species. Lichens mottle the trunk, which supports the adhesive roots of a Native Monstera, a hoya and a parasitic mistletoe. High in a fork of the tree, the bulb-like base of an Ant Plant hides a network of chambers sheltering a colony of ants.

Opposite: Strangler Figs create woody webs around host trees in Mossman Gorge, Daintree National Park.

Above right: The Golden Bowerbird, Prionodura newtoniana, is found in the mountain rainforests of the Daintree.

Previous pages
P18: *Hardy and Hook reefs, Great Barrier Reef Marine Park.*
P19: *Australia's Freshwater Crocodile, Crocodylus johnstonii.*

Location: 80 km (49.7 miles) north of Cairns via Mossman.

Climate: January is very humid and stormy, 23–31° C (73–88° F); July often has pleasant clear breezy days, 17–25° C (63–77° F); cyclone season December–April.

When to go: Anytime of the year, but the climate is most comfortable (cooler and less humid) May–September and March–July is the best time for wildlife watching.

Access: By road (2WD and 4WD roads and tracks) numerous vehicle guided tours from Cairns, Port Douglas and Mossman; vehicle hire available at Cairns. By air to Cairns International Airport. Boat tours available on the Daintree River.

Permits: Camping permit should be obtained from national parks offices in Cairns and Mossman.

Equipment: Camping gear, light wet-weather gear, footwear suitable for mud (boots are needed for off-track walking), sunscreen SPF 35+, hat, insect repellent, light clothing, swimming gear, vinegar for treatment of Box Jellyfish stings.

Facilities: There is a wide variety of accommodation on offer just outside the park. Boats are available for hire and there are also guided tours of the park. Vehicles can be hired from nearby towns. Walking trails, self-guiding park leaflets and picnic/barbecue areas. Information centre at Mossman.

Watching Wildlife: Fruit-eating birds most prevalent February–May. Aquatic wildlife easiest to observe in the waterholes of the dry season, July–October. November is a good time for spotting frogs.

Visitor Activities: Walking, wildlife watching, forest study, birdwatching, swimming (although visitors should beware of stinging Box Jellyfish October–May and crocodiles all-year-round), cruising on the Daintree River, snorkelling about the fringing reefs, 4WD touring.

Enclosed in a strangling net of fig-tree stems, a venerable giant of the forest has become a colossal staircase to the canopy 50 metres (164 feet) above.

A slight movement draws attention to a brownish animal half a metre (1 foot 8 inches) long, perched on a branch, with its long black-brushed tail hanging down and its stout forearms raised to pluck the succulent pinkish fruit of Bumpy Satinash. This rare sight is the mainly nocturnal Bennett's Tree Kangaroo having a final snack before retreating to its sleeping spot in the canopy.

Rainforest Chorus

As the forest gloom brightens with the rising sun, distinct footfalls reveal a powerful black ground bird – the Cassowary – around a metre (3 feet) or more high. It pushes its horny-crowned blue, purple and crimson head and neck through the trailing cords of a spiny Wait-a-while Palm as it works its way through the fallen fruit. Nearby, a flash of opalescent gold comes to rest on an amazingly tall woven twig structure – it is the Golden Bower Bird visiting its bower. Soon its ratchetting rattle of a call seems to signal other birds. The soft 'oom-oom-oom', the 'hook-coo-coo-coo-coo-coo' and the bubbling 'wompoo' of the Purple-crowned, Red-crowned and Wompoo pigeons merges with the liquid call of the opal-coloured Noisy Pitta and the ringing notes of the Golden Whistler.

Above: A lone mangrove survives on a beach in the Daintree National Park, south of Cape Kimberley.

Below right: Crinum Lilies, Crinum angustifolium, *and giant paperbark trees flourish on the coastal plain.*

Below: A regular feature on the Daintree River are Crocodile-watching cruises.

The plant sends its roots into the chambers and extracts its nutrient requirements from the food the ants bring in – just one of the many remarkable examples of the symbiosis that integrate the living rainforest community. All this before leaving the carpark!

Where Kangaroos Climb Trees

Moving quietly through the Daintree rainforest in the early light of morning can be highly rewarding. Among the rocketing trees with their fin-like buttresses, the floor is soft and damp. Sound is muffled by a thick mat of leaves smelling richly of decaying fungus and speckled with brilliant blues, crimson, purple, gold and vermilion – fallen fruit from Blue Quondong, Mossman Mahogany, Small-fruited Fig, Lemon Aspen and Scrub Breadfruit.

High in the crown of an emergent tree, Rainbow and Varied Lorikeets produce a cacophony of squabbling, strident screeches ringing through the treetops.

The rainforest and mangroves of the wet tropics are home to about 140 bird species – one day's spotting can top 50 species. A bonus sighting can be the stunning gold, emerald and black Cairns Birdwing, Australia's largest butterfly with a 15-centimetre (6-inch) wingspan.

Getting About the Daintree and Cape Tribulation Area

Graded self-guided walking tracks such as the Mossman Gorge Track and tracks into the Tribulation beaches and forest are accessible by ordinary vehicle. However, the track to the Bloomfield River, and Cooktown 72 kilometres (44.7 miles) further on, requires a 4WD vehicle. Fine accommodation and camping areas are abundant. Many commercially run guided tours are available from Cairns, Port Douglas and Mossman.

Daintree River boat excursions, and boat excursions to the Cape Tribulation beaches, including walks into the adjacent rainforests, are available from Port Douglas and from the Daintree River crossing.

Always remember – beware the hungry Saltwater (Estuarine) Crocodiles that inhabit the rivers and creeks.

Top: Smooth granite boulders line the Mossman River bed in the Daintree.

Above: Many rainforest trees like this Syzygium sp. are cauliflorous, producing blossoms on their trunk.

Far left: The Cooktown Orchid grows in the Cape Tribulation area.

Left: The rainforest's brilliant Green Pythons are nocturnal and arboreal.

LAWN HILL NATIONAL PARK

Canyons, Bones and Catacombs

Lawn Hill National Park lies 100 kilometres (62.1 miles) south of the Gulf of Carpentaria in the north-west corner of Queensland. Established in 1984, the park now covers 2,820 square kilometres (1,089 square miles) on the eastern edge of the spreading black-soil plains of the Barkly Tableland.

The most dramatic of the park's two distinguishing features is an imposing deep, red sand-stone gorge down which flows Lawn Hill Creek. The clear green waters are full of weighty Barramundi, Salmon-tailed Catfish and Freshwater Crocodiles, and are surrounded by lush tropical vegetation – quite a contrast to the semi-arid plant and animal communities of the park's plateau areas. In 1994, the park was given World Heritage listing in recognition of the importance of its second major feature – 100 square kilometres (38.6 miles) of fossil-rich limestone hills.

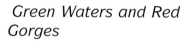

The Fossil Story

In 1976, scientists intrigued by a cow-sized marsupial fossil collected in 1900 at 'Riversleigh' cattle station next to Lawn Hill, made a series of dramatic fossil dis-coveries. Without exaggeration, millions of bones were uncovered bedded in the limestone, providing a brilliant picture of the landscape and wildlife evolutionary story of the area from 25 million years ago to modern times. So far, 88 animal families and at least 217 species have

Opposite: *Lily-covered Lawn Hill Creek is more like a river, even in the dry season when cascades shrink to tiny trickles.*

Above right: *The Crested Pigeon,* Ocyphaps lophotes, *shares Lawn Hill plateau with exquisite Spinifex Pigeons.*

been uncovered, including ancestral Platypus, Wombats and Koalas, pythons, bats, marsupial lions, crocodilians, huge freshwater turtles, giant flightless birds, cockatoos with large, crushing beaks, dasyurids and a weird animal humorously recorded as 'Thingadonta'.

This treasure-trove of fossils, probably the largest ever discovered anywhere, shows that, no matter what habitats they might use today, nearly every group of Australian terrestrial vertebrates apparently had its origins in the Gondwana rainforests. According to Professor Mike Archer, the leader of the Riversleigh researchers, 'our wildlife originated in a green cradle'.

Green Waters and Red Gorges

The last 130 kilometres (80.7 miles) into the park from the Wills Develop-ment Road crosses extremely dry, flat savanna landscape (no-one drives this road in the wet season as much of it is either underwater or composed of impassible greasy mud). After hours of heat and dust, the immaculate visitor reception area is an oasis of green lawns, with the largest Ghost Gum imaginable and a belt of inviting shade beneath a wall of massive Weeping Paperbark trees. Spaces between the papery trunks offer glimpses of deep green water overhung by *Pandanus*, while above the crowns of the trees, two red sandstone bluffs guard the mouth of the gorge.

A neat track leads to a wharf, which seems to be floating over a translucent green void until a silvery Salmon-tailed Catfish, almost one metre (3 feet) long, glides by below. Bands of striped Archer Fish, ready to shoot down unwary insects with a jet of water, cruise beneath dipping palm leaves. Canoes are available for

Location: Spread across the head-waters of the Gregory River, 200 km (124 miles) south-west of Burketown and the Gulf of Carpentaria, and 320 km (199 miles) north-west of Mount Isa.

Climate: May–November is the arid dry season, 25–43° C (77–109° F); November–April is the stormy, humid wet season with major flood-ing, 30–38° C (86–100° F). Cool, clear nights June–August.

When to go: From late April at the beginning of the dry season to around October is the most com-fortable time for walking although the area is accessible until December for river activities. Wildlife watching anytime.

Access: By road from Mount Isa via Barkly Highway and 'Riversleigh' cattle station (4WD advisable), 2WD from 'Gregory Downs'; roads are often closed for long periods during the wet season. Light-aircraft land-ing strip at Adels Grove.

Permits: Camping permit from parks office Lawn Hill or Townsville; early bookings advisable between Easter and October.

Equipment: Warm-weather cloth-ing, swimming gear, snorkelling gear, canoe, strong walking shoes or boots, daypack, first-aid kit, strong sunscreen, broad-brimmed hat, insect repellent, waterbottle, light camping gear, fuel stove.

Facilities: Limited park camping area, modern bathroom facilities, visitor information centre, ranger services, 20 km (12.4 miles) of walking tracks, boat launching site and landing, slipway access across waterfalls. Commercial campsite and store at Adels Grove, on the park boundary.

Watching Wildlife: The dry season is best as animals are drawn from the parched plateau to the limpid waters of Lawn Hill Creek.

Visitor Activities: Wildlife viewing and nature study, birdwatching, star gazing, walking, swimming, canoe-ing up the gorge, snorkelling.

Above: A *male Darter, Anhinga melanogaster, dries its feathers after fishing in Lawn Hill Creek.*

Above right: *The track on the Lawn Hill plateau around the gorge winds its way amongst Ghost Gums and Spinifex grass.*

hire at Adels Grove camp, and a paddler heading up the gorge to Indari Falls points out a Freshwater Crocodile sunning itself on the trunk of a fallen tree. Out of reach on the same snag a long-necked Darter perches with its brown-black wings hung out to dry. If this riverside is a relict of the lush environment of 10–20 million years ago, no wonder the animals of the nearby Riversleigh fossils flourished in the area.

The Red World of the Plateau

The walking track onto the plateau makes its graded way to the southern bluff top, winding past exquisite Ghost Gums. Hummocks of wiry blonde spinifex grass sheltering small marsupial mice and numerous reddish Ring-tail Dragons fill the gaps between large, angular, red sandstone blocks. This parched landscape is home to the beautifully marked Spinifex Pigeon, but apart from the occasional large Sand Goanna sunning itself, most land vertebrates are difficult to spot as they escape the heat of the day by retreating to cool hollows beneath boulders or to the river below.

The track winds its way along the gorge rim where narrow side gullies and defiles are crammed with fine-leafed Cabbage Palms. Below, hectares of purple and pink flowering waterlilies float on the long, green, limpid reaches of the pools. Like steps up the bed of the gorge, each pool ends in a low wall of tufa limestone over which the stream cascades into perfect

swimming places. In the coolness and shelter of the night, Rock Ringtail Possums forage about the rim rocks and palm gullies, avoiding hungry Olive Pythons.

Right: *Fossil ripples can be seen in the red sandstone rocks beside the track above Lawn Hill gorge.*

THE GREAT BARRIER REEF MARINE PARK

The World's Largest Coral Area

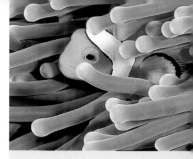

The Great Barrier Reef Marine Park off the coast of Queensland stretches for over 1,900 kilometres (1,180 miles) along the edge of the Coral Sea from the warm tropical waters of the Torres Strait, which separates Australia from Papua New Guinea, to the cooler waters south of Gladstone. Covering an area of 344,800 square kilometres (133,093 square miles), this unique park encompasses over 2,100 diverse and exquisite coral reefs and cays, 540 continental islands and a shimmering 'moat' of quiet water ranging in width from 24 to 290 kilometres (14.9–180 miles).

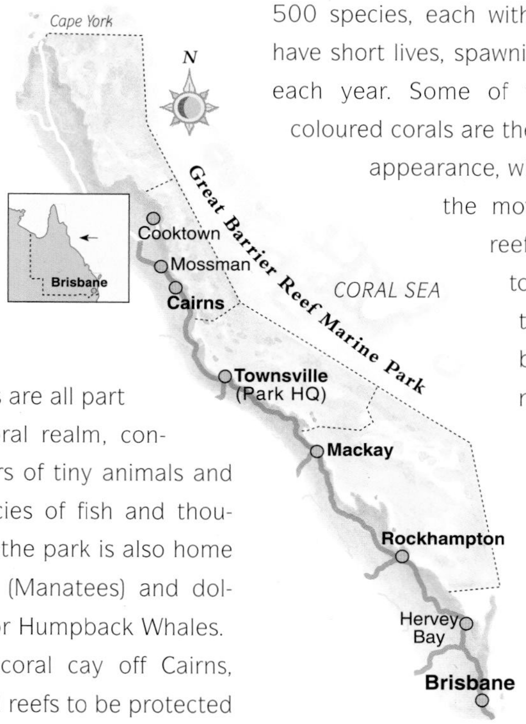

Linear, patch and fringing reefs are all part of the park's incredible living coral realm, constructed by unimaginable numbers of tiny animals and plants. Populated by 1,500 species of fish and thousands of species of invertebrates, the park is also home to thousands of turtles, Dugong (Manatees) and dolphins, and is a breeding ground for Humpback Whales.

In 1937, Green Island, the coral cay off Cairns, became the first of many cays and reefs to be protected as a national park. It was not until 1975, however, when the Australian government established the Great Barrier Reef Marine Park to protect the area from oil drilling, that the Reef as a whole came under protective management. This protection was reinforced in 1981 when the park received World Heritage listing.

Above right: *Symbiosis in action – an Anemone Fish nestles amongst the tentacles of an Anemone, immune to its poison.*

Overleaf: *The Whitsunday Group of mainland islands and their fringing coral reefs lie inside the Great Barrier Reef.*

The Exquisite Stone Makers

In a magical life alliance, the carnivorous coral polyp – a tiny colourful animal usually no larger than the head of a nail – is helped to live by even smaller plant cells within its body. Together they exist in vast colonies thriving on food filtered from the warm, clear sea water. Over 500 species, each with a particular colour and form, have short lives, spawning on only a few moonlit nights each year. Some of the most exotic and brightly coloured corals are the soft corals, almost plant-like in appearance, with rubbery 'fronds' that sway to the movement of the water. Hard or reef-building corals secrete a skeleton of calcium carbonate within their bodies. These skeletons become the foundation for the next generation of polyps.

Different coral species combine to create truly fantastic 'gardens' beneath the sea. Grottoes, cavernous spaces, great channels and piled-up masses of broken coral provide shelter, space and food for countless numbers of plants and sea creatures. These often rival the more spectacular elements of the reef in colour and form in order to hunt effectively or to remain hidden from predators and grazers. The striking Citron Coralfish, the Clown Triggerfish and the Red Emperor, for example, hide easily among the coral gardens.

Drowned Mountains and Coral Cays

Today's reefs have grown where Aboriginal people hunted kangaroos and Tasmanian Tigers (Thylacines) 15,000 years ago. The higher hills they climbed formed hundreds of continental islands as the sea levels rose. Here, as in

Map labels: Cape York · N · Cooktown · Mossman · Cairns · Brisbane · Great Barrier Reef Marine Park · CORAL SEA · Townsville (Park HQ) · Mackay · Rockhampton · Hervey Bay · Brisbane

Location: Off the Queensland coast stretching all the way from Cape York and the Torres Strait in the far north to Gladstone in the south, 400 km (248 miles) north of Brisbane.

Climate: Tropical, with dry, warm winters and hot, humid, wet summers. Intense sunlight, sea temperature above 20° C (68° F). Cyclone season November–April.

When To Go: Anytime, although high temperatures and humidity in summer mean the best months to visit are May–October. The climate is always humid and very warm to hot north of Mackay.

Access: By boat from Cooktown, Port Douglas, Cairns, Cardwell, Townsville, Airlie Beach, Shute Harbour, Mackay, Yeppoon, Gladstone, Seventeen Seventy, Bundaberg. Some islands are also accessible by plane or helicopter.

Permits: Check with the Marine Park Authority or any of the national parks offices in Cairns, Townsville, Mackay or Brisbane for current permit requirements.

Equipment: Sunscreen, broad-brimmed hat, swimming gear, snorkelling gear, light daytime clothing, warm clothing for evening, old sandshoes, fishing gear, zone notes and appropriate maps if sailing or boating, GPS equipment, transceiver, strong torch, effective water-safety gear.

Facilities: Over 40 resorts, full range of accommodation. High-speed catamaran ferries, light-aircraft charter available as well as regular services to some areas, self-sail hire yachts (bare boats), charter boats. Marine Park Authority aquarium and headquarters in Townsville.

Watching Wildlife: November–May for turtle nesting and terns, herons, Mutton Birds and Imperial Pigeons. Whale watching April–October; winter calving of Humpback Whales in reef waters.

Visitor Activities: Swimming, scuba diving, snorkelling, reef walking (permitted but not encouraged as the reef is a vast yet fragile living system), marine studies. Bird, whale and turtle watching. Boating, yachting, island exploration.

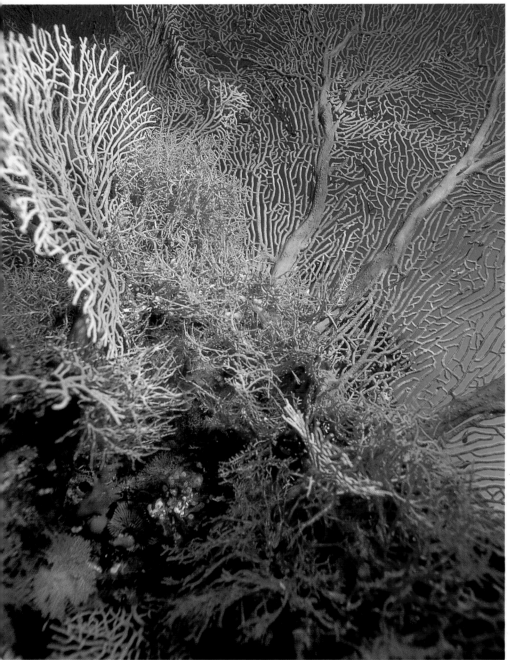

many places around Australia, the local Aboriginal people have stories and songs about being driven off their land by the rising seas. Usually hilly and well-wooded, some of these islands, such as Lizard and the Whitsundays, have been gradually surrounded by fringing reefs.

The lower rises, too small to survive as continental islands, were submerged and became the shallow foundations upon which true coral islands grew. Beginning as wisps of the whitest sand lying on labyrinths of patch reefs and shallow green lagoons, and later colonized by plants and animals, these fragile cays are especially vulnerable to the sudden onslaught of tropical storms. Vegetation on these islands can range from hardy creepers, such as *Convolvulus*, on a small coral cay, to the dense *Pisonia* forests of Heron Island, off Gladstone.

Exploring the Reef

In order to survive and thrive, polyps require a level of sunlight available only in clear salty water no deeper than 30 metres (98.4 feet) and water temperatures that don't drop below 17.5° C (64° F). This also happens to form the perfect environment for humans wishing to explore this magnificent undersea wonderland.

While the many islands throughout the park offer snorkelling and scuba-diving opportunities, the vast majority of visitors choose a day trip out of Cairns or Port Douglas. A typical reef excursion takes the visitor by

Top: *Bottle-nosed Dolphins,* Tursiops truncatus,*and their young are often seen frolicking inside the Reef waters.*

Left: *Orange Gorgonian fans and brittle pink Stylaster hydroids are two of a multitude of brightly coloured corals found in the vast Great Barrier Reef Marine Park.*

fast catamaran 50 kilometres (31 miles) out to a large pontoon that offers underwater coral- and fish-viewing facilities, a marked area for snorkellers to swim – with or without marine interpreters – scuba equipment for licensed divers, and even a restaurant.

Here on the outer reef, large bommies – towering coral masses – are alive with any number of beautifully marked Angelfish, liquid gold Damselfish, Parrotfish and Wrasse. Exquisite Clownfish shelter among the stubby stinging tentacles of anemones, while brilliant nudibranchs pulsate through the water. The lucky visitor may even spot a Green Turtle drifitng on the currents.

Returning to shore, boats may pass close to Michaelmas Cay – a special reserve for nesting seabirds where hundreds of Crested Terns, heads all pointing south-east into the wind, can be seen loafing on a spit end. Clouds of thousands of noisy Sooty Terns and Noddies swirl above the island during nesting season.

Sharing the Reef

The Great Barrier Reef Marine Park offers a whole world of birds, turtles and whales as well as a galaxy of fish, crustaceans, molluscs and worms and an incredible range of beautiful soft and hard corals. From Bundaberg to Cooktown there are many resorts and cities with accommodation and touring facilities but these are not the only demands on such an immense area.

Strict guidelines are required to ensure the sustainability of the Reef and its waters. Under policies set by the Marine Park Authority, the area is divided into management regions, each of which is zoned for a variety of uses – shipping and trawling, limited line fishing, commercial recreational activity, undisturbed appreciation and enjoyment, scientific research and restricted nature reserve.

Above: *A Loggerhead Turtle leaves its nesting beach on Heron Island.*

Below: *A Brown Booby and chicks – seabirds nest and rest on sand spits and cays.*

CARNARVON NATIONAL PARK

Stark White Canyons, Red Rock Art

Carnarvon National Park lies in the heart of Queensland, 724 kilometres (450 miles) north-west of Brisbane. Remote though the park may seem, visitors are drawn to Carnarvon's yawning white gorges, clear streams, fine forests, towering palms, tree ferns and vivid Aboriginal rock art. The park's spectacular chasms are built of white sand swept into the area by swollen rivers over millions of years. Compressed, cracked and eroded, the sandstones of today contain hundreds of great logs and branches from the ancient floods, many now just log-shaped holes in the cliffs. Beneath the beds of porous Precipice Sandstone impervious shales block water seeping through the sandstones, diverting it into Carnarvon Creek, maintaining a permanent flow.

Stretching 180 kilometres (112 miles) across Queensland's Central Highlands, part of Australia's Great Dividing Range, the park lies at the centre of a vast radial network of major rivers – the Thompson, Warrego, Maranoa, Dawson, Comet and South Burdekin. A small section of today's park was first protected in 1932. The last addition in 1990 created a total area of 2,980 square kilometres (1,150 square miles).

Life on the Canyon Floor

For the past 20 million years Australia has been caught in a gradually deepening drought, driving wildlife and plants from the drying interior to seek refuge wherever

Opposite: Precipice Sandstone encloses Carnarvon Gorge – a rich oasis of Cabbage Tree Palms and eucalypt forests.

Above right: Signs along this boardwalk help the visitor understand the Aboriginal artwork on the overhang wall.

wetness remains. Hence the incredible mix of plants that cluster around the permanent waters of Carnarvon.

The Carnarvon Creek Track begins at the boulder crossing where the creek is lined with River Oaks. Much of the walk passes through a towering forest of beautiful mauve-speckled Spotted Gums 50 metres (164 feet) high. Numerous stands of Cabbage Tree Palms rocket skywards, exploding in a mop of leaves beneath the eucalypt canopy. Young palms, Bracken Ferns and yellow hibiscus with plum-coloured centres rise through a floor of Bladey Grass. Here and there, the dinosaurian cycad *Macrozamia moorei*, spills its fiery red seeds from pineapple-sized cones.

Eastern Grey Kangaroos and Whiptail or Pretty-faced Wallabies, also abundant at the campground, can usually be seen bounding off into the bush. Along the track, gnawed seeds and holes chewed through tree bark to get at the sap are the only evidence of the area's nocturnal Brushtail Possums, Bush Rats, and Yellow-bellied Gliders. At night along this track, torchlight reflects from shining pairs of Greater Glider eyes, like stars high in the trees. The lucky visitor may also see this appealing black and white phalanger, with its long furry tail, making 100-metre (328-feet) glides to flowering eucalypt canopies. Vigorous movements and bickerings in the same flowering masses reveal Little Red Flying Foxes feeding. Nearby, Little Bent-wing Bats emit almost inaudible sonic squeaks as they pursue moths through the air, changing direction with incredibly rapid manoeuvres.

Short walks into side gorges reveal fascinating relict communities, such as the exquisite Moss Gardens and the ancient ferns that grow around Kamoodangie Creek

[Map]

Buckland Tableland Section

Salvator Rosa Section

Ka Ka Mundi Section

Carnarvon National Park

N

Carnarvon Gorge Section

Mt Moffatt Section

Visitor Centre

Moolayember Section

Brisbane

Location: Central highlands of Queensland, 245 km (152 miles) north of Roma and 240 km (149 miles) south of Emerald.

Climate: Hot, humid summers with violent storms; warm, dry, sunny winter days with chilly nights, some frosts. Spring is dry.

When to Go: Climate most comfortable from May–September or October; April–June best for wildflowers; wildlife, anytime.

Access: By road off the sealed Carnarvon Highway at 'Wyseby', 160 km (99.4 miles) north of Injune, 105 km (65.2 miles) south of Rolleston, then 43 km (26.7 miles) by clay road west to park headquarters. Access is difficult in wet weather. 4WD access only to Mount Moffatt section from Injune.

Permits: Camping permits from the parks office at the campground; five-day limit during school holidays. No campfires within park boundary.

Equipment: Strong walking shoes or boots, shorts for daytime, warm clothing for evenings. Binoculars, first-aid kit, sunscreen, hat, insect repellent in warmer months, swimming gear, camping gear, fuel stove and fuel, strong torch.

Facilities: Camping area with full facilities, graded walking tracks, backpack camping area at Big Bend, visitor centre, ranger services, Aboriginal art interpretation, self-guiding leaflets, park library. Carnarvon Gorge Oasis Lodge at park boundary, camping area on adjacent farm.

Watching Wildlife: Stream, woodland/forest and savanna communities in the park are rich with kangaroos and birds; plenty of nocturnal mammal activity.

Visitor Activities: Walking, climb to Boolimba Lookout for sunrise, nature and art study, bush camping, school-holiday programs.

Birds, Birds, Birds

From the tiny, delicate Red-backed and Variegated fairy wrens to the majestic Wedge-tailed Eagles drifting high on rising air, Carnarvon is a paradise for birdwatchers. At Sunrise Lookout, just as the sun is painting the Goombangie Cliffs across the valley golden, tens of thousands of screeching Rainbow Lorikeets pour from fossil log-holes in the escarpment cliffs to spend the day foraging for nectar in the flowers of the forests.

Large, deep-green King Parrots with brilliant emerald wing patches and crimson heads and breasts hurtle through the canopy. By the clear flowing creek the Azure Kingfisher is already quietly watching for any movement in the water – Sunfish, Jewel Perch or frogs – when a Platypus comes up for air after nuzzling the pebbly bottom in its search for freshwater shrimps and yabbies. And all around the creekside campground, the air is filled with a morning chorus of perhaps 50 bird species.

The Aboriginal Record

With plenty of food within easy reach, thousands of generations of local Pitjara Aboriginal people developed an incredibly rich spiritual and cultural life. Shot, poisoned or killed by foreign diseases during the 19th century, all that remains of the traditional owner/artists of Carnarvon is a near-permanent record of their occupation on the walls of many rock overhangs. Three of these are open to the public and are located not far from the information centre in the Carnarvon Gorge section of the park.

The Art Gallery is one of the finest expressions of stencilled art in Australia, with axes, pendants, hands, shields, boomerangs, animal tracks. The rock walls of the shallow cavern also exhibit painted freehand geometric designs, lizards and nests of eggs as well as hundreds of engravings. Balloon Cave holds stencils of large stone tomahawks and hands, some apparently providing sign language. Cathedral Cave is an awe-inspiring rock shelter, the ceiling and walls covered with hundreds of artworks among fossil log-holes. This cave is a full day return walk from the camping ground along the gorge.

Left: *The Wedge-tailed Eagle,* Aquila audax, *Australia's largest, is usually seen riding thermals above the gorge.*

Right: *Towards the track end at Cathedral Cave with its spectacular art-covered walls, Carnarvon Gorge becomes a narrow canyon with even narrower tributary canyons.*

FRASER ISLAND WORLD HERITAGE AREA

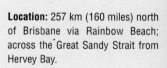

World's Largest Sand Island

Fraser Island is the largest sand island in the world – 1,840 square kilometres (710 square miles) in area, 125 kilometres (77.6 miles) long. Towering dunes covered in forest and wallum (tall tropical heath) rise to 244 metres (800 feet) above sea level from 200 metres. Scattered among the dunes lie 148 lakes of the purest water; gigantic blowouts of live dunes; clear streams edged with Piccabeen Palms and giant prehistoric ferns, *Angiopteris evecta*; forests of Satinay trees climbing 50–60 metres (164–197 feet) and lofty stands of Kauri and Blackbutt trees. The habitats are so rich that nearly half of Australia's bird species have been found on the island.

The island is 257 kilometres (160 miles) north of Brisbane, and separated from the mainland by Hervey Bay. In 1971, most of Fraser Island – 1,400 square kilometres (540 square miles) – was proclaimed part of the Great Sandy National Park, which also extends south along the mainland coast. The whole island was listed as the Fraser Island World Heritage Area in 1992.

So Much Sand, So Many Lakes

Fraser Island formed like a giant underwater sand eddy just off the coast, building with changing sea levels until the wind took over, sculpting dune upon dune.

Opposite: *Fraser Island, composed of massive mostly forested dunes, is the largest sand island in the world.*

Above right: *The island's Dingoes are said to be more purebred than Dingo populations elsewhere in Australia.*

Vegetation binds the surface of the island, but blasts of stinging sand from the beaches keep the dunes alive.

Occasional bushfires burned the protective cover, allowing the wind to scour out great hollows. Some of these were lined with vegetable matter and filled by rain and drainage to create lakes, a number of which perch many metres above sea level.

Lake Boomanjin, three kilometres (1.9 miles) across, is the largest perched lake in the world. Bowarrady Lake is noted for its wildlife, particularly for the friendly turtles, and Garawongera is a good habitat for waterbirds. The beautiful Lake McKenzie, the Blue Lake, offers superb swimming and excellent lakeside campsites.

Life on Fraser Island

Ten plant community types can be found on Fraser Island, ranging from pockets of tall, dense rainforest scattered throughout the island to the mangrove scrub of the west coast. Parts of the island support spicy-smelling, tall, open forests of giant Blackbutt, Tallow Wood and Red Bloodwood eucalypts. Typical Australian coastal plants such as acacias, geebungs, monotocas, banksias and tea-trees cover the island's dunes while numerous legumes, ground orchids and grasses carpet the forest floor.

Such varied forest makes 'night-spotting' – walking at night with a spotlight or strong torch in search of the island's elusive nocturnal creatures – very fruitful. Five species of phalangers and possums as well as Grey-headed Fruit Bats can often be spotted feeding at night among the blossoms and fruits of the forest canopy.

Map labels:
N
Sandy Cape Lighthouse
Brisbane
Harvey Bay
Orchid Beach
Wathumba
Fraser Island World Heritage Area
PACIFIC OCEAN
Lake Bowarrady
Moon Point
Cathedral Beach
Enchanted Valley

Location: 257 km (160 miles) north of Brisbane via Rainbow Beach; across the Great Sandy Strait from Hervey Bay.

Climate: Warm winter days, cool nights; hot and humid inland during summer (cooler on the sea front), stormy with intense rainy periods.

When to Go: Best during the cooler weather around May–September. Mosquitoes and march flies are also less abundant in the cooler months.

Access: By boat or barge from Urangan, River Heads and Inskip Point (Rainbow Beach); 4WD vehicle needed for island touring (care should be taken when driving on the beaches as vehicles can founder and sink in wet sand).

Permits: Vehicle permit for island use and camping permits available from parks offices at Brisbane, Maryborough, Noosa, Hervey Bay, Gympie and Rainbow Beach.

Equipment: Insect repellent, swimming gear, snorkelling gear, fishing gear, extra fuel, tyre pump and gauge (tyres should be slightly deflated for driving on the sand), tow rope, maps, first-aid kit and essential spares.

Facilities: Seven camping areas all with showers, drinking water and toilets, three with telephones. Other accommodation available at five-star Kingfisher Bay Resort, Dilli Village cabins, Eurong and Happy Valley. 4WD tracks, walking tracks.

Watching Wildlife: August–October best for whale watching from high shorelines; tortoises and birds at Lake Bowarrady; October–April for migratory waders on mud and sandflats; wildlife interpretation at Kingfisher Bay.

Visitor Activities: Nature study, beach and estuarine fishing, camping, walking, 4WD beach-touring, swimming, snorkelling, offshore-boating and lake canoeing.

Right: *Crested Terns stay by Fraser Island's many lakes when strong easterlies are blowing.*

Below: *Lace Monitors,* Varanus varius, *grow to two metres in length and often forage in island campsites.*

Below right: *The pure water of Lake Boomanjin, like most of Fraser Island's lakes, is coloured by the surrounding vegetation.*

The island also supports 60 species of reptiles, mainly harmless lizards including fat monitor lizards about 1.5 metres (5 feet) long, which can often be seen around campsites raiding for food. A sizeable population of Dingoes – reputed, in their isolation, to be the purest stock in Australia – keep a persistent predatory pressure on the island's many small ground mammals, as well as the Grey Kangaroos and Swamp Wallabies.

Birdwatchers are never disappointed on Fraser Island. Every year an average of 36,000 migratory waders feed and loaf on the mudflats. Eighteen species of raptors, including the grand White-bellied Sea Eagle and the Wedge-tailed Eagle, the largest of the Australian raptors, soar above and nest on the island. The island also supports an astonishing number of other bird species including 13 pigeon, 16 parrot, 11 cuckoo, 11 owl and nightjar and 25 honeyeater species.

Enjoying Fraser Island's Wonders

Fraser Island, like south-west Tasmania, the Myall Lakes and Kakadu, is only enjoyed as a national park today because prolonged public battles convinced governments that conservation was more desirable than commercial exploitation of these areas. Sand mining on Fraser Island is a thing of the past, today the dunes and lakes on the island give pleasure to thousands each year.

Most visitors explore the island by 4WD using Seventy Five Mile Beach, facing the Pacific Ocean, as the main thoroughfare. Eurong, just behind the beach at the 34-kilometre mark, is the gateway to the internal 4WD track system that provides access to the forests and lakes. Continuing up the beach there are several more villages and very beautiful campsites and seascapes. The beach ends at Sandy Cape at the northern tip of the island, a long way from anywhere.

LAMINGTON NATIONAL PARK

The Green Mountains

Established in 1915, Lamington National Park spreads across part of the 'Scenic Rim' of Queensland's MacPherson Ranges 90 kilometres (55.9 miles) south of Brisbane, the State capital. It is hard to believe that just 30 kilometres (18.6 miles) to the east of these wild 'green mountains' the gleaming skyscrapers of the Gold Coast line the Pacific Ocean.

The park spreads across the Lamington Plateau, encompassing a series of mountain ranges radiating north from the sheer cliffs of the New South Wales border like the spokes of a giant wheel. These are the north-western slopes of a massive extinct volcano 150 kilometres (93.2 miles) wide – its remnant core, Mount Warning (1,156 metres/3,792 feet), lies just south of the border in New South Wales. The deep gorges and canyons that separate the ranges are part of the ancient volcano's radial drainage system.

Most of the park is covered with rich storeyed rainforests laden with epiphytes and spiralling vines – Lamington was listed as part of the World Heritage Central Eastern Rainforest Reserve in 1986. Rugged and thickly vegetated, with spectacularly ancient trees, bubbling streams and beautiful waterfalls, Lamington's 206 square kilometres (79.5 square miles) must be explored on foot as no roads traverse the park.

Luxuriant Rainforests

Lamington is a wet plateau with ranges over 1,000 metres (3,280 feet) high catching the moisture-laden

Above right: Fungi such as this Collybia sp. *transform the rainforest's organic matter into essential lifegiving nutrients.*

south-easterly winds off the Pacific. Bubbling mountain streams and rivers fed by the deluge plunge into gorges – the magnificent Coomera Falls pours out of a small opening in an amazing green wall of ferns and vines.

The park's misty high tops are crowned with a cool-temperate rainforest of gnarled Antarctic Beech trees – some over 2,000 years old – dripping with white Beech Orchids, ferns, lichens and mosses. Emerging from the mist zone, taller, warm-temperate Coachwoods, with their leathery grey trunks, mingle with clusters of tree ferns.

Lower on the ranges, the warmer subtropical rainforest displays a luxuriant diversity. On the ground, masses of ferns, gingers and palms join small trees awaiting a break in the canopy high above before they begin growing rapidly towards the light. Massive Strangler Figs smother their host trees with a woody web, climbing ever upwards. Throughout, the forest is fringed in the fuzzy green of epiphytes, and tonnes of Crows Nest Ferns, Elkhorns and Staghorns create a hanging garden high in the tops of Giant Stinging Trees and towering Booyongs.

Creatures of the Forest

The soft, haunting cooing of feeding fruit pigeons high in the canopy, including the gorgeous Wompoo, explains the pattering of falling fruit and kernels. Brightly coloured pigeons like this one, along with screeching Crimson Rosellas and King Parrots, splash the forest with colour. A pile of warm decomposing leaf litter a metre (3 feet) high shows where the Brush Turkey is incubating its eggs. Echoing up from the floor of a gorge, the mimicking calls

Map labels:
To Canungra
Romeo Lahey Memorial
Binna Burra Lodge
Stairway Falls
O'Reilly's Green Mountains Guesthouse
Cominan Lookout
NEW SOUTH WALES
Brisbane
Lamington National Park
N

Location: 107 km (66.5 miles) south of Brisbane via Canungra to Binna Burra; 115 km (71.4 miles) south of Brisbane via Canungra to 'Green Mountains'.

Climate: May–September, cool to cold nights, most days warm and clear; October–March, humid and warm to hot, many misty days, storms; December–March, heavy tropical rain.

When to Go: Anytime, although the cooler, drier months of winter and spring are best for walking.

Access: By sealed roads to Binna Burra and 'Green Mountains' from Brisbane, Beaudesert and the Gold Coast, however, the narrow mountain passes are unsuitable for caravans or large trailers.

Permits: Camping permits are required and are available from the ranger station at Binna Burra.

Equipment: Strong mud-proof shoes or boots, wet-weather gear, waterbottle, binoculars, warm jacket, insect repellent.

Facilities: Privately run accommodation, camping and picnic areas at Binna Burra and Green Mountains; information centre at Binna Burra; 150 km (93.2 miles) of graded walking tracks throughout the park including a wheelchair access track. Tree-top boardwalk at Green Mountains, trailside picnic areas, ranger services.

Watching Wildlife: Wildlife sightings in the park are opportunistic, although kangaroos and wallabies are usually to be found on the grassy areas around the centres of Binna Burra and Green Mountains. Colourful parrots and other birds are fed from the centres and often gather in large numbers.

Visitor Activities: Walking on the many tracks carved into the thick rainforest of the park, wildlife spotting, stream and geological studies.

of the Albert Lyrebird ring through the trees amid the rush of falling water. Shy Platypus are abundant but rarely seen in the mountain pools and streams.

Night in the rainforest is the time of the large Powerful Owl, watching in silence for movement before plummeting, talons ready, towards a small hunting Brown Antechinus, a gliding phalanger or a rainforest Ringtail Possum. The Red-legged and the Red-necked pademelons, small secretive wallabies found around the edges of the rainforest, are too large for the Powerful Owl.

Walking the Park

Any of the walks throughout the park's superb track system exhibit the same cool, humid, air and any visitor who plunges into the forest is greeted with the unmistakeable, and not unpleasant, smell of damp fungus. No sound emanates from footfalls in the deep leaf litter – a world that is home to astronomical populations of invertebrates and speckled with white, golden, Prussian blue and orange fungi. Venture into the forest at night and some species even exhibit an eerie luminous glow.

Over 150 kilometres (93.2 miles) of these tracks can be accessed from either Binna Burra at the eastern end

Above: *Elabana Falls lies on the headwaters of Canungra Creek.*

Top right: *The Eastern Water Dragon is often seen beside creeks and falls.*

Right: *Coomera Creek is home to the beautiful blue Macpherson Range freshwater crayfish,* Euastacus.

of the Border Track, where accommodation is available in the famous Mountain Lodge, or from the equally famous O'Reilly's guesthouse ('Green Mountains') at the western end. Both places have clearings where hundreds of wild parrots, many Regent Bower Birds and some wallabies come to be fed every day. A raised walkway through the forest at O'Reilly's provides a bird's-eye view of the world as it traverses the canopy 30–40 metres (98.4–131 feet) up among the fringes of Staghorns and the 'hanging gardens' of orchids.

Either base offers camping areas for there are only rare opportunities to camp anywhere deep in the forests. All 14 tracks in Lamington are day walks or less. The full Border Track along the Scenic Rim from Binna Burra to O'Reilly's is a very long day walk that offers magnificent views south into New South Wales and across the ranges towards Mount Warning National Park.

Top: *The timid Red-necked Pademelon,* Thylogale thetis, *rarely ventures beyond the forest to feed near campsites.*

Above right: *The Border Track between Binna Burra and 'Green Mountains' offers a spectacular rainforest experience.*

Right: *Male King Parrots,* Alisterus scapularis, *and green-headed females are common in the forest canopy.*

Far right: *A fragile* Hygrophorus sp. *fungi is one of many species growing in the damp leaf litter of the rainforest floor.*

NEW SOUTH WALES

On 22 August 1770 Captain James Cook formally took possession of the eastern coast of Australia in the name of His Majesty King George III of England, thus setting aside thousands of years of occupation by Australia's Aboriginal people. From that point in time, the western half of the continent was known as New Holland and the eastern half as New South Wales. Today, a much-reduced New South Wales of 801,600 square kilometres (309,418 square miles) is bordered by Queensland to the north and Victoria to the south, with a coastline stretching for 1,900 kilometres (1,180 miles) in between.

Even with Queensland and Victoria excised, New South Wales is probably the most diverse area on the continent. The climate ranges from subtropical in the north to temperate in the south, with the spectacular Kosciuszko National Park sheltering much of the State's subalpine highlands. Most of the State's moisture is driven by onshore winds, south-westerly winter weather and tropical weather overshooting from the north in summer. Aridity increases towards the parched continental centre. The subtropical rainforest and wet eucalypt forest of Dorrigo National Park on the north coast escarpment lies in sharp contrast to the incredible dunescapes of Mungo National Park in the State's far west.

Five physical regions extend from the Pacific Ocean westwards to the South Australian border: the coast and coastal plain; the eastern highlands or Great Dividing Range, running the length of the entire east coast of Australia; the western slopes of hills and residual ranges; the inland plains of the Murray–Darling river system; and, west of these, the arid hills, ranges and dunelands of the desert country.

While the New South Wales and southern Queensland coast is Australia's most densely populated area, national parks protect much of the adjacent mountain country and many of the State's magnificent beaches. The first so-called 'national park' in the world, the Royal National Park, lies on the coast just south of Sydney, the State capital. The Myall Lakes National Park in the north protects some of the finest coastal lagoons in New South Wales and, 700 kilometres (435 miles) northeast of Sydney, deep in the Pacific Ocean, lies spectacular Lord Howe Island, a World Heritage Area that shelters the southern-most coral reefs in the world.

DORRIGO NATIONAL PARK

World Heritage Rainforests

D orrigo National Park, 40 kilometres (24.8 miles) inland along the road to Armidale from Urunga on the New South Wales north coast, encompasses a thickly vegetated area of spectacular rainforest and wet eucalypt forest. Spread across the upper catchment of the north arm of the Bellinger River (Rosewood Creek), the rugged park of 79 square kilometres (30.5 square miles) is cut by numerous small streams cascading off the Dorrigo Plateau.

High rainfall, fertile volcanic soils and a landscape with an altitudinal range of over 970 metres (3,182 feet) rising from the coastal plain, has produced highly varied communities of plants and animals. The park was established in 1927 and protects the last remnants of the dense rich forests of the once vast Dorrigo Scrub. The area's world significance was acknowledged in 1986 when it became part of the Central Eastern Rainforest Reserves World Heritage Area.

A Green Refuge

The closed canopy of a rainforest shelters a moist, shaded world of immense beauty – a natural hothouse

Opposite: *Thick rainforest covers the Dorrigo escarpment.*

Above right: *The Australian King Parrot.*

Previous pages
P42: *Dramatic sandstone cliffs in the Blue Mountains NP.*
P43: *Artificial water supplies mean Red Kangaroo populations have increased across the inland plains of New South Wales in ever greater numbers.*

of permanent high humidity draped with epiphytic ferns, orchids and lianas. Dorrigo rainforests range from subtropical to warm temperate types and contain a large number of species competing for the limited light and nutrients. The temperate rainforest in particular – a relict of a long chain of forests that ran from Tasmania to north of Cairns along the escarpment of the Great Dividing Range – contains many species of Gondwanan origin. The enclosed valleys and eastern slopes of the wet escarpment provided refuges for pockets of rainforest to survive through the many severe drought cycles of the past 20 million years. Many of Australia's drought-resistant plants, such as the arid land grevilleas, have their origins in rainforest.

The Dynamic Rainforest Centre

From the village of Thora, the road through the park climbs Dorrigo Mountain, rising through eucalypt forests and subtropical rainforest to warm-temperate rainforest at the top of the pass. Suddenly the rainforest ends and the road emerges onto a bright sunlit rolling plateau, once supporting dense rainforest, now covered with Kikuyu grass. The Dorrigo World Heritage Rainforest Centre is perched at the forest edge with its Skywalk running out from the escarpment over the canopy. The display in the centre provides an explanation of the way the rainforest system fits together as well as describing ways to experience this park and others of this World Heritage Area.

Warm Temperate Rainforest

A stroll along either the Wonga Walk, Blackbutt Track or the Rosewood Creek Track takes the visitor deep into the forests. The Rosewood Track drops off the plateau from

Location: Along the coastal escarpment 60 km (37.3 miles) southwest of Coffs Harbour; 75 km (46.6 miles) east of Armidale.

Climate: Winter nights are cool with occasional frosts; summers are hot and humid with afternoon storms; rain is particularly likely in late winter and summer; fogs occur on the escarpment.

When to Go: Cooler temperatures in autumn, winter and spring make these the best seasons to visit; October–March is hot and humid.

Access: By car via the coast road from Urunga; by air to Coffs Harbour or Armidale then by car. Coach tours from Coffs Harbour.

Permits: There are no official car camping campsites and therefore no permits are required; bushcamping while bushwalking is free.

Equipment: Light clothing, strong water-resistant shoes, wet-weather gear, hat, waterbottle.

Park Facilities: Rainforest Visitor Centre, Skywalk (a wooden walkway that runs straight out over the forest canopy from edge of the escarpment offering visitors a spectacular bird's-eye view of the park), another boardwalk that winds down through the canopy from the top of the escarpment, picnic areas, graded walking tracks, toilets, cafe for refreshments and light foods.

Watching Wildlife: Opportunistic sightings along tracks. Canopy birds can be spotted from the boardwalk, Scrub Turkeys and Pademelons (wallabies) are often seen about The Glade picnic area.

Visitor Activities: Walking, bushcamping, picnics, rainforest study.

Right: *Platypus Creek flows amongst the tree ferns and Coachwoods of Dorrigo's warm-temperate rainforest.*

Below: *Armillaria asprata is one of the many fungi found growing on moss-covered logs in the damp forest floor of Dorrigo NP.*

the Never Never Picnic Area, first through tall eucalypts, then into warm-temperate rainforest to become immersed in tree ferns. The straight, leathery-grey trunks of Coachwoods spearing to the canopy 40 metres (131 feet) up contrast with the deeply furrowed grey bark of the Crabapple. Silent footsteps crush spicy smelling Sassafras leaves and, beyond the massive leaf-mound incubator of a Brush Turkey nest, the Dorrigo Waratah of the family *Proteaceae* splashes the bush with crimson. The Waratah's close relationship with plants of Africa and South America is a reminder to the visitor of Australia's ancient Gondwanan heritage.

Subtropical Rainforest

Further down the scarp, the track swings onto a warmer north-east face. Almost immediately, Strangler Figs begin to replace the Coachwoods, creating spectacular webbed towers as they engulf their supporting tree. Nearby, the Giant Stinging Tree has plate-sized soft green leaves

loaded with potent stinging hairs. Bright Flame Tree flowers and the reddish, young leaves of the Red Cedar in spring provide splashes of colour. Large-leafed Tamarind trees and Piccabeen Palms add contrasting textures. Other trees with wide-spreading buttresses include the Yellow Carabeen and the Booyong. The huge, buttressed trunks are swathed in climbing ferns, Pothos Vine, Birds Nest Ferns and Elkhorns. Amongst the massive feathery banks of epiphytes hang orchids such as the Orange Blossom Orchid while, down below, numerous colourful fungi and flowering Ginger and Walking Stick Palms grow from the rich damp litter of the park's forest floor.

Forest Fauna

Most mammals in Dorrigo, particularly the Brushtail and Ringtail possums, are nocturnal, although the secretive Red-necked Pademelon (a wallaby) can be seen feeding at the edge of picnic areas. Large Carpet and Diamond Pythons move quietly about all levels of the forest.

No matter where you are in Dorrigo, birds are rarely far away – spectacular Crimson Rosellas and King Parrots frequently flash through the canopy and, on the ground, the Superb Lyrebird, Brush Turkey and brilliantly coloured Noisy Pitta search for food amongst the leaf litter. Acrobatic Rufous Fantails hunt insects above the creek while Platypus sun themselves on creekside boulders; bombed with fruit and seeds falling from feeding Topknot, Brown, Wompoo and White-headed Fruit pigeons high in the overhanging canopy.

Left: *The Skywalk allows visitors to the World Heritage Rainforest Centre at Dorrigo NP to walk above the treetops.*

LORD HOWE ISLAND WORLD HERITAGE AREA

The Ultimate Paradise

Only 15 square kilometres (5.8 square miles) in area, this drop in the Pacific Ocean 770 kilometres (478 miles) north-east of Sydney was first sighted by humans on 17 February 1788. From its dramatic volcanic peaks to its pristine beaches and aquamarine waters, the island was covered with subtropical vegetation dominated by four species of endemic palms. Without any major predators, island wildlife was totally unafraid of the visiting humans who gathered large numbers of animals to feed the starving convict colony at Sydney.

The island was settled in 1836 and proclaimed a forest reserve in 1878. Five years later it was declared a botanic reserve to preserve the endemic Kentia Palm, core of the island's income. A Permanent Park Preserve was established in 1981 covering 80 per cent of the island. In 1982 UNESCO placed 1,463 square kilometres (565 square miles) of the Lord Howe Island Group of islands, associated coral reefs and marine environments on the Register of World Heritage Properties.

Millions of years of waves, rain and wind have etched the extinct volcano into a remarkably beautiful landscape. The island's twin peaks, Mount Lidgbird (777 metres/2,549 feet) and Mount Gower (875 metres/2,870 feet), drop sharply to limpid waters with magnificent fringing reefs. The wild drama of these cloud-making peaks at the southern end of the island and the spectacular cliffs of Malabar at the northern end contrast with the rolling emerald hills of the centre. The settlement spreads across these cleared hills and while there is no clear town centre, the focus is the opalescent lagoon on the western side of the island.

Immaculate pale coral beaches line both sides of the central section of the island, while the beaches of 'secret' coves at Boatharbour, Rocky Run and near Little Island are composed of smooth shining basaltic boulders. Millions of grotesquely shaped needle-sharp pinnacles rise from parts of the coast and lagoon, etched over time from ancient coralline dunes.

Map labels: Mt Eliza, Neds Beach, North Head, Visitor Centre, N, Valley of Shadows, Blackburn Island, Cobby's Corner, Lord Howe Island World Heritage Area, Rocky Point, Little Island, Mt Lidgbird, Mt Gower, Sydney

Fire and Water

About seven million years ago, lava began oozing from one of the Earth's many hot spots 2–3,000 metres (6,560–9,840 feet) beneath what is now the Tasman Sea. Half a million years later, the growing pile of volcanic material finally broke the surface of the ocean and Lord Howe Island was born – a major shield volcano built by lava flow and violent eruptions.

Above right: Wedgetailed Shearwaters or Muttonbirds, Puffinus pacificus, nest on the island through the summer.

A Living Laboratory

About a third of the island's 228 plant species are endemic. The raw materials for colonization arrived by wind and water, and were also carried to the young volcano by birds from Australia, New Zealand and the island chain to the north of Lord Howe. Riding the warm East Australian Current, which terminates in the Tasman Sea around Lord Howe Island, warm marine vertebrates and invertebrates – such as worms, corals, molluscs and fishes – arrived as eggs, larvae and mature animals.

Location: 770 km (478 miles) north-east of Sydney surrounded by the Tasman Sea (Pacific Ocean).

Climate: Subtropical; wet and windy winters. Temperatures range from 10–26° C (50–79° F). Cloud obscures the tops of Mt Gower and Mt Lidgbird most days of the year.

When to Go: August–April. Best from October–February.

Access: By air from Sydney, Brisbane and Norfolk Island; luggage weights are strictly limited.

Permits: No permits are required as camping is prohibited.

Equipment: Diving, snorkelling and fishing gear, swimming gear. Light clothing for summer days, wet-weather gear, warm clothes for evening, strong walking shoes, old sandshoes for exploring littoral zones, binoculars for birdwatching.

Facilities: Guesthouses and self-contained units are available for rent on the island, but accommodation is limited so it is advisable to book well ahead. Boats can moor safely inside the reef. Twelve walking tracks around the island range from easy to extreme; some interpretive signs are provided. Boats may be chartered for dive and fishing expeditions. Bicycles are available for hire. General stores, museum, information centre, post office.

Watching Wildlife: Opportunistic sightings on the network of tracks across the island. Shearwaters arrive from Siberia and the North Pacific in September to breed; Providence Petrels can be seen around Mt Gower, Red-tailed Tropic Birds about the mountains and the cliffs between Kims Lookout and Malabar. Woodhens are often seen in Little Island palm forest, 4 pm fish-feed at Neds Beach.

Visitor Activities: Walking, cycling, swimming, surfing, snorkelling, scuba diving. Rock, bay and boat fishing. Birdwatching, mountain climbing (guide required), boating.

Settling on Lord Howe Island in its isolation, these species initiated the evolution of new lines of species that were better adapted to the island's peculiarities of environment. Biodiversity was on the increase in this living laboratory.

Soon oceanic birds, such as the Red-tailed Tropic Bird trailing its fabulous scarlet feathers, Shearwaters and Providence Petrels took up residence along with vagrants blown off course such as Currawongs, Golden Whistlers, Silver Eyes and the long-billed rail.

Today's Lord Howe Island Woodhen is the direct descendant of the first rail migrants. The very large population of 1788 was reduced by hungry settlers to 25–30 birds by 1969. An intensive breeding program and a reduction in the numbers of rats has seen this friendly brown bird recover from near extinction to a population of 200 in 1998. It can be seen on Mount Gower and in the palm forest near Little Island.

The Human Side of Lord Howe Island

In 1789, a year after the island was first discovered, whalers working the 'Middle Ground' of the Tasman Sea came ashore for water and to plunder birds, turtles and vegetation. It wasn't until 1833, however, that settlers arrived bringing domestic cattle, pigs, goats and horses and began developing a small and quite unique community.

The impact of humans, feral pigs and goats on wildlife was catastrophic and, after concern was raised in 1868, the first of many scientific visits occurred the following year. The island's first rats, survivors from the wreck of the SS *Makambo* in 1918, aggravated the situation, eating their way through palm seed, endemic ground nesting birds and invertebrates. Within a few

Top: The spectacular walking track along the top of Malabar Ridge on the northern edge of Lord Howe offers a magnificent view south across the whole of the island.

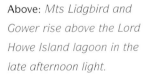

Above: *Mts Lidgbird and Gower rise above the Lord Howe Island lagoon in the late afternoon light.*

Right: *Diligent conservation efforts saved the Lord Howe Island Woodhen,* Gallirallus sylvestris, *from near extinction.*

years, five species of ground birds were extinct, and the release of mainland owls to eat the rats simply added another predator instead of solving the problem.

Today, the island is administered by an enlightened Lord Howe Island Board, which, along with the New South Wales National Parks and Wildlife Service, manages the Permanent Park Preserve and the island's wildlife. The pigs have been destroyed, the goats have been reduced to a small population and the rats are being controlled with carefully marked poison baits.

Visiting Paradise

Twelve walking tracks, ranging from easy to extreme, allow the visitor to thoroughly explore every nook and cranny of this magnificent island. Viewpoints, beaches, bays, rock platforms and forests await discovery. The walk to Goathouse Cave on Mount Lidgbird offers sensational views of Lord Howe and Balls Pyramid – a dramatic rock that rises 551 metres (1,807 feet) vertically from the sea to a sharp pinnacle, home for many seabirds such as petrels. Only the track up Mount Gower is quite difficult – walkers must be accompanied by an approved island guide. Nearer the settlement, the track to Malabar follows the cliffs through soaring numbers of spectacular Red-tailed Tropic Birds.

Snorkelling in the lagoon and about the reefs is also popular. Experienced locals lead scuba-diving excursions and boat and fishing trips around the island and to Balls Pyramid. A range of accommodation is available but bed numbers are very limited. A carrying capacity of 393 has been set by the Management Board – a crucial move in maintaining the natural values of Lord Howe Island.

Top: *Large numbers of noisy Red-tailed Tropic Birds,* Phaeton rubricauda, *can be seen flying in sweeping circles around the cliffs and mountains of the island at any time of the year.*

Above: *Mount Lidgbird looms above Rocky Run Track near the south-east tip of the island.*

Left: *A catamaran rests on Old Settlement Beach across the lagoon from cloud-capped Mount Lidgbird and Mount Gower.*

MUNGO NATIONAL PARK

Sands of History

Established in 1979, Mungo National Park protects a surrealistic dunescape and dry lake system in the semi-arid heart of south-western New South Wales. The dunes around the eastern margin of dry Lake Mungo have been sculpted by wind and rain into dramatic features known as 'The Walls of China'. The 417-square-kilometre (161-square-mile) park is extremely flat and ranges between just 64 and 100 metres (210 and 328 feet) above sea-level.

Around 15,000 years ago this area of the vast Murray–Darling river basin was part of the chain of elliptical Willandra Lakes – a shallow glistening paradise for wildlife. Since the 1960s, scientists studying the ancient sand and clay layers in the lakesides and dunes have discovered a remarkable history of human occupation – campsites and human remains more than 30,000 years old, and much older prehistoric animal fossils. In 1981, the listing of the Willandra Lakes Region World Heritage Area – of which Mungo is a critical element – recognised the global significance of the archaeological and geomorphological features of the area.

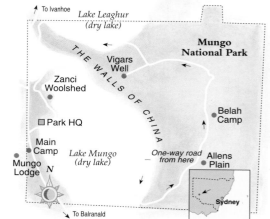

A Trip Back in Time

Any visit to Mungo is a fascinating trip back in time – a reconstruction of the history buried in its sands. Imagine

Opposite: *Active sand dunes form the unstable eastern edge of the lunette which borders dry Lake Mungo.*

Above right: *A Desert Mole Cricket skitters across Mungo's baking dunes, avoiding the sharp eyes of hunting Kestrels.*

the scene 45,000 years ago. The climate is warm and humid; the sun has just risen above the high eastern lunette dunes covered with dark green conical Callitris native pines and a mix of Pittosporum, mallee and Rosewood. Black Box trees line the lake shoreline. Down a well-worn trail, a family of bullock-sized diprotodons, plod to the water … a shivering of weeping grey-green Rosewoods draws attention to massive blunt-faced Procoptodons, giant browsing kangaroos. Several grazing, hare-sized Bettongs, small macropods, lift their heads as a Thylacine or Tasmanian Tiger, lopes down to the lake. A scraping sound followed by a shower of sand reveals the presence of an active Hairy-nosed Wombat making its burrow more comfortable for daylong sleep. (Fossils of all these and other animals are common here.)

Across the water beyond the reedbeds, a cacophony of honking, quacking, rasping and whistling sounds signals the presence of flocks of ducks, Magpie Geese, Coots and Brolgas – the grey Australian crane. On a muddy bank a large varanid lizard, four metres (13 feet 2 inches) long, is tearing apart a wallaby carcase. The shoreline mud is a continuous frieze of footprint impressions telling the story of life and death in this dynamic place, punctuated by bleached bones and teeth settling in to become the fossils excavated today.

Human Footsteps

Ancestors of today's traditional owners, the Barindji people, arrived some time before 30,000 years ago and preyed on this boundless source of food. They experienced the

---

Location: 120 km (74.5 miles) to Balranald, 109 km (67.7 miles) to Mildura on the Murray River, 88 km (54.7 miles) to Pooncarie on the Darling River.

Climate: The park experiences scorching summers when 40°+ C (104°+ F) is common and cool winters. Rain when it happens, usually in winter; rain closes road access. July–September is magnificent.

When to Go: April–October but not during rain when roads become inaccessible. Best during the cooler months of July–September.

Access: By gravel and clay roads from Balranald, Mildura, Ivanhoe and Pooncarie. The Pooncarie road is the closest to the sealed roads. Tours of the park are available from Mildura on the Murray River.

Permits: Bookings to stay in the 'shearers quarters' from parks office, Buronga; park entry is free.

Equipment: Warm winter clothing, strong shoes, broad-brimmed hat, light covering clothing for summer, waterbottle, sunscreen, first-aid kit.

Facilities: 67-km (41.6-mile) self-guided tour drive loop, ranger services, visitor information centre, historic woolshed and other buildings; Grasslands Nature Walk with self-guided signage; accommodation in 'shearers quarters' and nearby 'Mungo Lodge'; unpowered camping area.

Watching Wildlife: Red and Grey kangaroos very common, lizards and snakes common. Great numbers of Galahs, Corellas and other parrots gather near the ground tanks at sunrise and sunset. Finches are common about water. Wedge-tailed Eagles throughout the park.

Visitor Activities: Walking and car touring. Wildlife watching and bird-watching. Archaeological, geomorphological and historical studies, Aboriginal heritage.

gradual changing of the climates and maintained a cultural memory, a 'dreaming', about the now-dry lakes as places of glorious abundance.

Favourite foods were mussels, Murray Cod weighing up to 30 kilograms (66 pounds) and Golden Perch, which fed on mussels, crayfish and frogs. The people established a lore from the 'dreaming', which ruled their relationships with Mungo and with each other. Today's Barindji people are closely involved in setting the policies for managing Mungo, particularly its Aboriginal places.

Mungo Today

Today, Lake Mungo is parched. Western Grey and Red kangaroos and Emus feed in their hundreds across the grasses of the dry lake while huge flocks of pink and grey Galahs wheel overhead. Shingleback skinks and many other lizards, including perhaps 10 species of tiny velvety geckoes, some beautifully marked, scuttle about the hot dry land. Although four of Mungo's many snake species are listed as dangerous, the largest reptile likely to be spotted is the harmless Carpet Python which can reach 4 metres (13 feet) in length.

There is a vast spaciousness and silence at midday, when the heat of the pitiless sun drives animals underground or towards shade; at midnight, the timeless glittering southern sky exposes our fragile existence. The rusted iron of the historic deserted shearing shed built by Chinese labour 135 years ago creaks in the wind, a reminder of the area's pre-park role as a sheep station.

In the cool after first light, a car leaves a dust cloud across the lake on its way to the lunette dunes where visitors piece together the fascinating clues of earlier times, or photograph the exquisite modelling of eroded mini 'grand canyons' and clay spires. The visitor centre and resident archaeologist help to explain the story buried in the sands, but it is the simplicity and timelessness of Mungo landscapes that grip the imagination.

Above: *The eroded clay beds of Mungo's 'Walls of China' contain major deposits of human and prehistoric fossils.*

Left: *Butter Bush,* Pittosporum sp., *is a lunette plant.*

Below left: *Pretty Round-leaf Pigface grows in salty soils.*

Below: *Little Corellas,* Cacatua pastinator, *flock near water beside an old windmill – a relic of Mungo's pastoral days.*

MYALL LAKES NATIONAL PARK

Sweeping Surf Beaches and Shimmering Lakes

The Myall Lakes National Park, established in 1972 after a major battle over mineral-sand mining, protects 316 square kilometres (122 square miles) of glorious coastal features. Located 236 kilometres (147 miles) north of Sydney and 75 kilometres (46.6 miles) from Newcastle, the Myall Lakes are a chain of three great shimmering coastal lagoons rimmed by wide sandy shallows and broad areas of wetlands – habitat for large numbers of local and migratory waterbirds and waders.

Tall smoothly rounded ridges covered with a mosaic of eucalypt forest and sub-tropical rainforest run down to the park's lagoons from the west, while high forested dunes to the east form the barrier that separates lagoon from ocean. Long curving beaches at the face of the dunes stretch between the spectacular Yacaaba, Dark Point, and Big Gibber headlands and Treachery Head – the 'drowned' extensions of the inland ridges. The Myall River runs quietly through tranquil swamps forested with Cabbage Tree Palms and Swamp Oaks, draining the chain of lagoons into Port Stephens.

Lake Life

The Myall Lakes form the most extensive brackish to freshwater lagoon system on the New South Wales coast. These lagoons are a rare layered aquatic ecosystem with denser saline waters lying beneath a fresher upper strata. Typical marine fish, such as Flathead and Whiting, live on the saline bottom, Silver Bream live in a wide range of salinities, while Mullet range into completely fresh water. The Broadwater and Boolambayte lakes are saline while the largest lake and the furthest from Port Stephens, the Myall, is almost fresh.

Such a gradient in salinity means that the lakes support a wide range of aquatic plants and animals as well as providing the specific range of habitats required during the life cycle of School and Tiger prawns. For a period of about 10 days after the full moon in February – the 'February dark' – vast numbers of prawns run down the Myall River from the lakes to the sea. Five-tonne hauls in the river nets are common.

Canoeing is one of the best ways to explore the lakes, allowing the visitor to drift among Pelicans and numerous Black Swans without disturbing the wonderfully placid waters. Early mornings and late afternoons provide magic times gliding beneath spreading Broad-leafed Paperbark branches and gnarled trunks, coming upon unsuspecting Coots, Swamphens and Black Bitterns, or finding yourself the sudden centre of panicking schools of Whiting and Mullet.

Another popular way of exploring the lakes is to hire a houseboat at Buladelah on the Myall River. A quiet anchorage in a secluded bay offers the perfect opportunity for observing the resident Teal, Black Duck and Black Swans, while a fishing line soon draws in a Silver Bream or Luderick for dinner. Before using power boats, check restriction zones with the park service.

Opposite: Paperbark Trees, Melaleuca quinquenervia, surround The Broadwater, most brackish of the Myall Lakes.

Above right: The Laughing Kookaburra, Dacelo novaeguineae, is found throughout southern Australia.

Location: 16 km (9.9 miles) east of Bulahdelah or up the Myall River from Hawks Nest.

Climate: Cool, wet winters; warm to hot summers, humid with thunderstorms; dry, warm autumns.

When to Go: Anytime but the climate is best from August–April; wildflowers are at their best from late July to December.

Access: By sealed road via Bulahdelah, Bungwahl and Tea Gardens; 4WD via beach from Tea Gardens to Big Gibber; by boat via Myall River and from ramps at Bulahdelah, Mungo Brush, Bombah Point, Bungwahl and Violet Hill.

Permits: Park use and camping fees collected on the spot by rangers.

Equipment: Water safety gear if boating, swimming gear, fishing gear, light clothing, insect repellent, binoculars. There is no firewood available in the park so visitors should either bring their own wood or bring a fuel stove and fuel.

Facilities: Camping from Mungo Brush to Bombah Point. Caravan, tent sites and cabins at Myall Shores. Full accommodation available at Tea Gardens, Hawks Nest and Bulahdelah. Numerous shoreside picnic areas throughout the park. Houseboat hire at Buladelah, boat hire at Tea Gardens.

Watching Wildlife: Waterbirds are easily spotted at anytime; honeyeaters flock to the park during the flowering season in late July–December. Wallabies and Grey Kangaroos are seen on grassed areas, Dingo sightings opportunistic, night spotlight walks for possum and phalanger observations.

Visitor Activities: Birdwatching, lake and river snorkelling, boating, canoeing, swimming, walking, wildflower study, lake and ocean fishing.

Walking the Park

The park offers many kilometres of bracing beach and dune walking, with access from Mungo Brush campsite, the Big Gibber 4WD track and Seal Rocks. Immediately behind the frontal dunes, tall, open forests of Blackbutt and superb Sydney Red Gum spread above Grass Trees, *Macrozamias* and numerous ground orchids including the tall Hyacinth Orchid, many greenhood species, the Duck Orchid and the surreal Bearded Orchid. Grey Kangaroos, Red-necked Wallabies and Swamp Wallabies are common and diggings of Spiny Anteaters are seen around old logs and about ant nests. These forests also have a resident Dingo population.

Apart from the nature trail into the rainforest at Mungo Brush, the park has few tracks and visitors are free to walk through open bushland. Take particular care when wandering through the expansive heathlands, which have a glorious flowering season from July to October. Aromatic Boronias, wattles, Pink-flowered Paperbark, white nectar-rich Tea Tree, bright pink milkworts, masses of soft Flannel Flowers, large Golden Glory Peas, Heathy Parrot Peas, purple Flag Lilies, blue *Caladenia* orchids, exquisite Pinkie Orchids and, later, the large Christmas Bells are just a few of the plants of the wet and dry heaths. Perhaps the best access to the heathlands is from the 4WD track which runs from Bombah Point to the Seal Rocks road.

Offshore, a number of islands are part of the park while others are very special nature reserves. Cabbage Tree Island, the Gould Nature Reserve, protects the only known nesting area of the Gould Petrel. From its high summit, Yacaaba Head, part of the park near Hawks Nest and Port Stephens' northern headland, offers some of the finest seascapes to be found anywhere.

BLUE MOUNTAINS NATIONAL PARK

The Glory of Sandstone

The Blue Mountains National Park, established in 1959 and covering 2,470 square kilometres (953 square miles), is just one of a crescent of 10 sandstone national parks around Sydney – breathing space for a city of over four million and for even more visitors seeking rest and inspiration.

Two river systems, the Grose and the Coxs, have cut a labyrinth of valleys and gorges a thousand metres (3,280 feet) deep into the plateau. The main road and rail route west from Sydney, 45 kilometres (27.9 miles) to the east, runs along the plateau-top on the divide between the two catchments. For 60 kilometres (37.3 miles) the Great Western Highway winds through 18 towns perched on the edge of Blue Mountains wilderness, giving access to numerous bushland walking tracks and park roads. Lookouts along the cliffs provide magnificent vistas across the 'blue' forested valleys, rimmed with glowing gold sheer sandstone 'walls' 200–300 metres (656–984 feet) high.

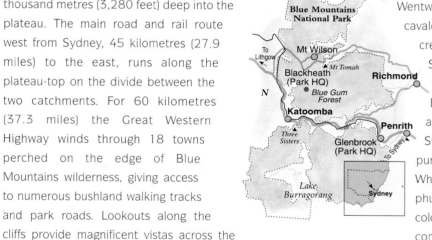

Wildflowers on the Sandstone

Almost all of the fertile shales have been eroded from the Blue Mountains high country, leaving sandstone, which is very deficient in phosphates. Sandy soil from the sandstone supports a great variety of heathland and woodland plants adapted not only to low-phosphate levels but also to drought. Many of these plants have leathery wax-covered leaves, such as those of the Scribbly Gum, Bloodwood and Waratah, or small spiky leaves, such as those of the Native Fuchsia, or long, narrow

Above right: *A Jewel Beetle perches on the fiery flower of the spiky Mountain Devil, or* Lambertia formosa.

leaves, such as those of the banksias and the Mountain Devil. All burn very rapidly in a bushfire but after thousands of generations living with fire they have developed survival adaptations such as insulated buds and seeds.

For the visitor, the most attractive characteristic of the heathlands and woodlands is the brilliant flowering spectacle for many months each year, particularly in the area between the towns of Wentworth Falls and Mount Victoria. The cavalcade of colour starts in July with the cream and golden hues of the wattles. Soon spots of crimson appear – the Native Fuchsias and Mountain Devils. By September, the heath and understorey is ablaze with Pink Swamp Heath, delicate Boronias, purple *Hoveas*, Flag Lilies, exquisite White Beards, numerous epacrids, sulphur-flowered Geebungs and brightly coloured bush peas. The grand finale comes in November when the Waratahs, New South Wales' floral emblem, light up the woodland between Katoomba and Mount Victoria with their great, tightly packed, crimson flowerheads.

Wild Blue Valleys

Many visitors come to the park for the spectacular and easily accessible views. In most other parks, tracks begin at the bottom of mountains and views must be earned by a hard trek to the top. In the Blue Mountains, tracks begin at the top, often at the lookouts themselves and usually not far from the Great Western Highway, before diving down cliffs and gullies towards the blue valley floors.

Some of the most enchanting vistas are those across the broad Jamieson and Grose valleys from cliffed rims at Echo Point, Evans Lookout, Govetts Leap, Anvil Rock, Perrys Lookdown and Wentworth Falls. Near most lookouts,

Location: On the plateau between the Great Dividing Range and Sydney, the eastern boundary is 45 km (27.9 miles) west of Sydney; the western boundary is 101 km (62.7 miles) east of Bathurst.

Climate: Warm to hot summers with storms; cool to cold winters, damp and misty, occasional light snow; many clear days throughout.

When to Go: Spring, summer and autumn for the upper mountains where winters can be chilly; spring and autumn for the lower mountains where summers can be hot.

Access: By vehicle or train to Glenbrook, Wentworth Falls, Katoomba, Medlow Bath, Blackheath or Mount Victoria from Sydney; by bicycle or road to trail heads; bus transport in Katoomba city.

Permits: Not required in the upper Blue Mountains. A park fee is payable at the Glenbrook entrance to the park in the lower mountains.

Equipment: Warm, waterproof clothing. When walking in the bush wear strong footwear and take walking track guidebooks, large-scale maps, matches, waterbottle, binoculars and a strong torch.

Facilities: Katoomba and Blackheath offer the full range of accommodation, from youth hostels to expensive hotels, as well as eco-tour lodges, takeaway food and restaurants; Katoomba offers supermarkets and car hire as well as canyoning, abseiling and other adventure tours.

Watching Wildlife: Kangaroos and wallabies can be spotted in the evening and early morning at Euroka and the Blue Gum Forest; parrots, honeyeaters and possums are common throughout park. Lyrebirds can sometimes be seen in damp forest and woodland areas. Spotlighting is rewarding.

Visitor Activities: Walking; birdwatching; botanical, geological and geomorphological studies; abseiling, canyoning, rock climbing.

long, wispy streams of water fall from hanging swamps – wet plant communities containing numerous surprises in miniature such as insect-eating sundews and masses of pink-flowering *Sprengelia*.

Among the glistening vegetation by the waterfalls is the very rare endemic dwarf conifer *Microstrobos fitzgeraldii*. In the moist valley below, tree ferns, Coachwood and Lillypilly trees form a green canopy of rainforest almost crowded out by lofty Sydney Blue Gums, Peppermint Gums and Turpentine trees reaching for the sky. It is said that the oils in eucalypt and other sclerophyll leaves vaporize to give the mountains their atmospheric blue. Certainly this drier forest covers slope after increasingly blue slope, slipping quietly into a distinctly blue distance accessible only on foot.

Top: *The famous Three Sisters, Echo Point, Katoomba.*

Left: *Trigger Plants are named for the pollen-loaded stigma triggered when a nectar-seeking insect 'tickles' the flowers.*

Mountain Wildlife

The Superb Lyrebird is common in the park forests and woodlands and makes its presence most felt from May through to November when the male carols to its mate from a network of about a dozen dancing mounds throughout its breeding and feeding territory. Its repertoire is incredible and includes the calls of the numerous honeyeaters that abound during flowering periods, Pied Currawongs, Golden Whistlers, treecreepers, King Parrots, Crimson Rosellas, Yellow-tailed Black Cockatoos, Scarlet Robins, Grey Shrike Thrush and many other local birds, as well as artificial noises such as chainsaws, axes and train whistles.

Many species of skink, gecko, dragon and varanid are very common in the mountains, while snakes such as the Red-bellied Black (mildly venomous), Tiger Snake and Death Adder (highly venomous) are rarely encountered. From April to August almost all reptiles are in hibernation. Most marsupials are nocturnal and cryptic, with the exception of the Grey Kangaroo, Red-necked Wallaby, Swamp Wallaby and the monotremes – the Echidna,

Top: *The park's Eastern Water Dragon,* Physignathus lesueurii lesueurii, *is common in streamside habitats.*

Above: *The magnificent Waratah, New South Wales' State emblem, produces flowers with heads 5" (12 cm) in diameter.*

Right: *The waterfall at Blackheath Glen is one of many in the Blue Mountains easily accessible by walking tracks.*

found anywhere at anytime, and the elusive Platypus, which inhabits the cold larger streams. At night, Brushtail and Ringtail possums, as well as the forest phalangers – the Greater, Squirrel, Yellow-bellied and Sugar gliders – may be spotlighted in parts of the forests.

Tracks Into the Wilderness

Visionary trackmakers in the late 19th and 20th centuries created a network of picnic areas and walking tracks on both sides of the Great Western Highway, particularly from Blackheath, Katoomba, Leura and Wentworth Falls. More than 50 tracks were constructed along remarkable routes fantastic in their conception, including some with steps cut down sheer rock faces.

Notable tracks around Blackheath include the Grand Canyon, Rodriguez Pass and those about Govetts Leap. The Giant Stairway and Federal Pass walks from Katoomba and the National Pass and the Overcliff Track near Wentworth Falls are all breathtaking. Tracks through wilderness include those through the Upper Grose Valley and the Wollangambe Wilderness, as well as those heading towards the Coxs River, Mount Cloudmaker and Kanangra Walls. Closer to home, the Mount Solitary and Blue Gum Forest walks are equally spectacular.

ROYAL NATIONAL PARK

Australia's First

The words 'national park' appeared in law for the first time anywhere in the world when The National Park, on the southern fringe of Sydney, was proclaimed in 1879. It was established by Sir John Robertson 'to be the lungs' of the rapidly growing and sickness-ridden city. The park has more than doubled in size to 151 square kilometres (58.3 square miles) and, in 1954, became Royal National Park under the patronage of Queen Elizabeth II. Today it is one of 10 national parks forming a wide crescent around the city.

Located 32 kilometres (19.9 miles) south of the Sydney CBD, the city's suburbs crowd around the park and over four million visitors a year enjoy its remarkably natural landscapes. Much of the park is wildflower-rich heath and woodland-covered sandstone plateau, rising from the waters of Port Hacking in the north to 500 metres (1,640 feet) above sea-level near Wollongong in the south. Twenty-one kilometres (13 miles) of sculptured sandstone cliffs, coves, bays and beaches form the park's dramatic eastern boundary, while the body of the park is cut by the magnificently entrenched gorge of the Hacking River.

Fine Forests and Spacious Moors

The sandstone 'tops' of Royal National Park have shallow infertile soils giving rise to low woodlands of

Opposite: *The park's Coast Track offers fabulous views such as this one across Garie Beach, Era and Burning Palms.*

Above right: *This official 1879 map of the National Park was probably the first map of a 'national park' in the world.*

Bloodwood and contorted, bleached Scribbly Gums that seem to dance across the landscape. A fantastic variety of flowering heathy shrubs including Red and Pink Spider Flowers, numerous acacias, Sydney Boronia and Heath-leaved Banksia stream out from beneath the woodland to form the wide Curramoors running down to the sea cliffs. During flowering periods, the heathlands are alive with chattering crowds of honeyeaters feeding on the nectar. These include the New Holland, Brown-headed, White-cheeked, White-eared, Tawny-crowned, and Eastern Spinebill honeyeaters.

In late spring, around October, when the Dwarf Apples are in snowy flower, an exotic aroma leads the visitor to the charming Native Rose. By November the woodlands and forest are lit by the crimson bursting flowers of two of the most spectacular of the park's plants – the Giant Lily with its flower stems rising four metres (13 feet 2 inches) into the air and the Waratah, with its large, compact, flower-head glowing crimson through the bushland.

The Heart of the Matter

Running north through the park's heart, the Hacking River has worn right through the sandstone of the tops into underlying shales, which have broken down into rich soils. This fertile, damp environment carries a dense warm temperate rainforest through which wanders Lady Carrington Drive – one of the park's early roads and now a walking track. Here, the visitor will hear the call of the Superb Lyrebird and may even see it or the Satin Bower Bird and plump Wonga Pigeons among the tree ferns, Lillypillys, Coachwoods, Sassafras and Red Cedars.

Location: 32 km (19.9 miles) south of the Sydney Central Business District on the Princes Highway, stretching down the coast from Port Hacking in the north to just north of Wollongong in the south.

Climate: Cool, damp winters; warm to hot summers with storms and bushfires. Autumn is usually warm and dry, while spring is changeable.

When to Go: Anytime. Wildflowers are best in spring and these attract thousands of honeyeating birds. Walking is best in autumn and winter, especially in the less shaded areas of the park .Swimming and snorkelling in summer when the ocean is warmest. The park is sometimes closed when fire danger is high. After fires some areas of the park may be closed to allow the vegetation to regenerate.

Access: By train to Engadine, Heathcote or Otford; by ferry from Cronulla railway station across Port Hacking to Bundeena; by car and bicycle via Audley, Waterfall, Stanwell Tops and Bundeena.

Permits: Pay car entry fee at park entrance; camping permit and bookings from visitors centre at Audley.

Equipment: Strong walking shoes or boots, camping gear, fishing gear, diving or snorkelling gear, swimming gear.

Facilities: Bike and boat hire, picnic facilities, visitor information centre. Guided walks, talks and tours. Kiosk open weekends.

Watching Wildlife: Marine invertebrates on rock platforms along the coast walk; possums, kangaroos and deer (introduced early in the 20th century) often seen from Lady Carrington Drive, Cedar Track and Wallumurra Track; honeyeaters on the heath, especially in spring.

Visitor Activities: Walking, swimming, wading, camping, fishing, diving, snorkelling.

are home for the uncommon Yellow-bellied Gliders and Greater Gliders. Brushtail Possums, one of the great survivors of human settlement, are common throughout the park and easily spotted at night. A population of Javan Rusa Deer, introduced early in the 20th century, effectively maintain themselves on coastal grassy areas.

Spectacular Walks

Many park visitors drive straight to the easy access picnic areas of Garie Beach and Wattamolla, but one of the best ways to experience the park is to walk the Coast Track, which runs for 27 kilometres (16.8 miles) from Bundeena on Port Hacking in the north to Otford railway station in the south.

Along the way a number of delightful backpack bush-camping places near beaches, inlets and in the forest provide a surprisingly wild experience for a park so close to such a big city. Burning Palms Beach, Marley Beach and Curracorang are among the special sites that make this walk the finest in the park. A short distance from Curracorang Creek, the remains of Aboriginal camps near seven rock overhangs provide evidence of the original occupants of the area.

Other walks that pass through spectacular flowering and scenic areas include the Uloola Track from Waterfall to Audley – where the visitor information centre is located – the Karloo Track from Heathcote to Audley, the Little Marley Trail and The Forest Path.

The Cedar Track offers a great introduction to this forest as it winds its way past the great white trunks of the Sydney Blue Gums, piercing the rainforest canopy. The Wallumurra Track from Lady Carrington Drive to Sir Bertram Stevens Drive passes through all of the park's plant communities from rainforest and tall open forest of Turpentines and Blackbutts to Scribbly Gum woodlands and the heathlands along the coast.

Ringtail Possums thrive in the rainforest understorey trees, while the tall eucalypts about lower McKell Avenue

Opposite: *The Coast Track near Eagle Rock reveals dramatic sandstone cliffs between Wattamolla and Garie Beach.*

Above left: *Over 700 species of flowering plants on the Curramoors heathland burst into flower from July–October.*

Right: *Nocturnal phalangers such as this Greater Glider,* Petauroides volans, *can be found in the park's protected woodland and forest habitats.*

Far right: *Echidnas, or Spiny Anteaters, are found throughout Australia in habitats ranging from desert to alpine areas.*

KOSCIUSZKO NATIONAL PARK

The Snowy Mountains

At 6,471 square kilometres (2,498 square miles), Kosciuszko National Park is the largest park in New South Wales and among the largest in the world. Ranging from 300 metres (984 feet) above sea-level at the lower Snowy River to 2,228 metres (7,308 feet) at Mount Kosciuszko, Australia's highest mountain, the park contains the most extensive expanse of alpine land on the continent.

Well-worn mountain ranges creased with wooded slopes and valleys roll away into the distance, alpine meadows covering the higher lands in carpets of summer flowers. Boulder streams, frost-heaved soils, string bogs and geometrically patterned ground are signs of earlier periglacial conditions. At the coldest times, a small area of glacial activity plucked out bowl-like cirque valleys and today there are five glacial lakes and a number of moraines in the area.

Following the Great Dividing Range 160 kilometres (99.4 miles) north from the Victorian border, part of which follows the Murray River, the park shares a section of its north-eastern boundary with the Australian Capital Territory's subalpine Namadgi National Park. Kosciuszko is 50 kilometres (31 miles) by road from Canberra, the nation's capital.

The park also encompasses the important catchments of the Snowy, Murray and Murrumbidgee rivers and is the centre of Australia's skiing industry. Thousands of people visit the snowfields each year for magnificent cross-country skiing through the snowgums as well as an excellent downhill experience. These critical catchment and recreation areas began to be protected from decades of destructive grazing in 1944, when the area became a State park. In 1967, the Kosciuszko lands became a national park and cattle grazing finally ceased in 1972.

Opposite: Autumn mist drifts around Snow Gums, or White Sallys, Eucalyptus pauciflora, in the park's subalpine areas.

Above right: Alpine or Hoary Sunray, Helipterium albicans.

The Living Mountains

Australia's subalpine and alpine regions are comparatively small in area and so isolated from other such regions that the biogeography, genetics and behaviour of Kosciuszko's flora and fauna is of world interest. Of particular note are the Broad-toothed Rat and the rare marsupial Mountain Pygmy Possum, the endangered Corroboree Frog, the beautifully adapted Alpine Water Skink, the unique lake fish *Galaxias findlayi* and chameleon-like Kosciuszko Wingless Grasshopper.

Vegetation in the park ranges from stands of one of the world's tallest flowering plant species – the Alpine Ash – in the lower areas of the park up through the contorted Snow Gum woodlands of the treeline into the alpine heaths, herbfields, bogs and fens, and sod-tussock grasslands and on to the feldmark of the most exposed places on the high tops.

Most beautiful in summer are the herbfields of buttercups, starry-white Snow Daisy, pale pink *Euphrasias*, masses of deep pink Trigger Plants and golden Buttons. Of the 185 plant species in the alpine zone alone, many need to mature rapidly in the short growing season. The most beautiful is surely the magnificent Anemone Buttercup, which gets away to a flying start in spring, beginning to grow beneath the edges of the melting snowdrifts.

Location: Extends 160 km (99.4 miles) north from the Victorian border; 450 km (280 miles) south-west of Sydney, 70 km (43.5 miles) west of Cooma.

Climate: Cold winters, four months of snow; warm summers with skin-burning sun (blizzards can occur midsummer); autumn and spring are quite variable.

When to Go: Skiing and snow holidays, June–early October; walking and wildflowers, November–April; lake fishing anytime.

Access: By road into park from Albury/Khancoban, Tumut, Cooma/Jindabyne, Adaminaby, Tumbarumba; by air to Cooma then car. Ski resorts by road from Jindabyne (Mt Blue Cow only accessible in winter by Skitube railway from Bullocks Flat or Perisher Valley, and Charlotte Pass by snowcat from Perisher Valley). Coach trips run from Sydney and Canberra.

Permits: Park entry fee, daily or seasonal, from park entrance or parks office Jindabyne; inland fishing licence from parks office.

Equipment: Blizzard-rated downhill and cross-country ski gear, low-temperature camping gear, wet and cold weather clothing, large-scale maps, first-aid kit. Vehicles must carry well-fitted snow chains in winter months (available for hire).

Facilities: Ski tows and chairlifts, roadside picnic areas, visitor information centre in Jindabyne. Accommodation within park at Thredbo, Charlotte Pass, Perisher Valley, Smiggins Hole, Guthega, Sawpit Creek; outside park in Jindabyne, Berridale, Cooma, Adaminaby and Tumut.

Watching Wildlife: Throughout the park. Kangaroos at Sawpit Creek, Platypus in Tumut, Eucumbene, Thredbo, Murrumbidgee, Indi and lower Snowy rivers.

Visitor Activities: Downhill and cross-country skiing, walking, trout fishing, wildflower and wildlife study, birdwatching, picnicking.

Top left: *Cross-country skiing is a glorious way of exploring Kosciuszko's vast Snow Gum woodlands in the wintertime.*

Left: *Summertime in the park is a great time for walking – a wire mesh protects the fragile alpine areas from damage.*

Above: *The Blue Lake is one of Kosciuszko's few cirque lakes – bodies of water held in bowls of rock, or cirques, plucked out of mountaintops by moving ice millions of years ago.*

Despite the area's biogeographic isolation, many of the Kosciuszko National Park's alpine meadow plant species have relatives in the Northern Hemisphere. The violet *Veronicas*, pink and lilac Eyebrights, buttercups, blue Ajugas, Violas and the Poa Snowgrass all have their northern counterparts. Over the past 20 million years or so, these plant genera have probably 'mountain-hopped' southwards through New Guinea as the Australian continental plate drifted closer to Asia.

Below the Treeline

Below 1,850 metres (6,068 feet), trees become dominant. Low woodlands of Snow Gums soon become mixed with the taller Candlebarks, Mountain and Ribbon gums to form the wet sclerophyll forest of the lower altitudes. Stands of giant Alpine Ash are clearly visible on high mountainsides as brownish-green patches. Some 30 species of eucalypt have adapted to a range of environments from the treeline to the lowest levels of the park.

Above: *White Snow Daisies,* Celmisia sp., *bright yellow Buttons,* Craspedia sp., *and purple Eyebrights,* Euphrasia glacialis, *line the track to Mount Kosciuszko.*

Top right: *A Kosciuszko plant sparkles with frost in early summer.*

Bottom right: *The nocturnal Common Brushtail Possum,* Trichosutus vulpecula, *dwells in woodlands.*

There are few genera anywhere in the world that show such adaptability and this is the reason why the eucalypt, restricted to Australia and New Guinea before 1800, is now the most widespread cultivated tree genus on Earth.

Wildlife in the Park

Kosciuszko National Park is home to many marsupials, among them the Mountain Pygmy Possum, restricted to habitat above 1,400 metres (4,592 feet) and thought to be long extinct before being discovered in a mountain hut in 1966. Another rare animal, the Broad-toothed Rat, lives in the mixed subalpine wet heath and sphagnum habitats. Grey Kangaroos, Red-necked Wallabies, Swamp Wallabies and Wombats are often seen feeding in the camping and picnic areas, particularly at dusk, but the park's possums are nocturnal and difficult to spot.

The common though elusive Platypus might be spotted in the larger pools of the park's rivers and large streams, particularly early in the morning and at dusk as it forages the bottom for yabbies, worms and other invertebrates, coming up for air at regular intervals.

Late in spring, millions of Bogong Moths migrate from northern New South Wales and Queensland to gather beneath the boulders of the park's high country. Aboriginal people once travelled long distances to gather and feast upon these nutritious fat-rich insects.

Left: *The Snowy River drains the slopes of Kosciuszko's Main Range.*

Below left: *The Common Wombat,* Vombatus ursinus, *dwells in burrows beneath the subalpine snows, as it feeds it pushes the snow aside like a miniature bulldozer.*

A Park for all Seasons

Summer provides the opportunity to experience the park as a whole with walks from Thredbo to Kosciuszko, Charlotte Pass to Blue Lake and the Main Range or from many of the excellent roads. These can be short rambles, strenuous day walks or long backpack wilderness walks. Some people enjoy simply driving along the roads and picnicking, others spend their time fishing the Snowy Mountains Hydro-Electric Scheme lakes for Brown and Rainbow trout.

In winter, cross-country skiing through a sparkling winter wonderland among twisted, ice-glazed Snowgums powdered with fresh fallen snow is a magical way to explore the park. Routes from Kiandra, from Jagungal to Perisher and The Chalet, and from Thredbo Village to Kosciuszko and south to Victoria provide many hundreds of classic kilometres of spectacular cross-country skiing. Ski resorts at Thredbo, Charlotte Pass and Perisher-Blue – which incorporates Perisher Valley, Smiggins Hole, Blue Cow and Guthega – provide numerous downhill skiing opportunities.

VICTORIA

Victoria, occupying the south-east corner of the continent, is the most southern of Australia's seven mainland States and Territories. At 227,600 square kilometres (87,854 square miles), or three per cent of Australia, it is about the same area as Great Britain. The varied coastline of 1,800 kilometres (1,118 miles) extends west in an arc from Cape Howe to the South Australian border, with sweeping beaches, lagoons and bays, rocky headlands and the breathtaking cliffs and sea stacks of Port Campbell National Park.

The Great Dividing Range pushes into the north-east of the State from New South Wales, following the arc of the coast through central Victoria and ending in the semi-arid mallee scrub country of the Murray River basin in the west. Much of the State's northern boundary follows the mighty Murray west from the Australian Alps. A rainshadow north of the Great Divide contributes to the arid nature of the north-west, although rainfall is high to the south and east of the mountains. The spectacular Alpine National Park, Victoria's largest, spreads loosely across the highest parts of these ranges, protecting the Snow Gum woodlands, Mountain Ash forest and grasslands of the State's alpine and subalpine country. At the tail-end of the Great Divide, in the west, the Grampians National Park attracts thousands of people every year to its rugged wooded landscape and wildflower displays. Mount Bogong (1,986 metres/6,514 feet) in the Victorian Alps – an offshoot of the highest part of the main range – is the State's highest peak.

Port Phillip Bay, sheltering the State's capital, Melbourne, pushes deep into the southern coast. South-east of the bay, visitors flock to the spectacular scenery and wildlife of Wilsons Promontory National Park, the southernmost point of the Australian mainland. In eastern Victoria, the lofty wet open forests of the wide Gippsland Plains lie behind the massive sand bars and lagoons of Ninety Mile Beach and its extensions. Even further east, pushed up against the New South Wales border at Cape Howe, the wilderness of Croajingolong National Park, with its richly flowering coastal heaths, has been designated a World Biosphere Reserve.

ALPINE NATIONAL PARK

The Skyline Trail

In 1989 an untidy knot of plateaux, ridges, outlying mountain masses and high plains along the Great Dividing Range was brought together to become Victoria's Alpine National Park. Stretching for over 200 kilometres and covering a total of 6,731 square kilometres (2598 square miles), the park links up with the Kosciuszko National Park in New South Wales. Together with Namadgi National Park in the Australian Capital Territory, a huge area of continuous national parks – 14,260 square kilometres (5,504 square miles) –protects virtually all of Australia's mainland alpine and subalpine country.

The Alpine – parts of which are only 220 kilometres (137 miles) north-east of Melbourne, the State's capital city – is easily the largest of Victoria's national parks. Its vast highlands shelter struggling feldmark communities and alpine meadows as well as sweeping panoramas of rolling grasslands and hundreds of square kilometres of Snow Gums, their writhing white trunks falling into tremendous forested hollows and gorges. Here, the rush of gathering streams forms a muffled background to the ringing call of the Superb Lyrebird and Mountain

Opposite: *Mount Buffalo, on the edge of the Victorian Alps, offers a spectacular view south across the Alpine NP.*

Above right: *Winter wetness enhances the reddish bark of this twisted Snow Gum,* Eucalyptus pauciflora.

Previous pages

P70: *Entrance to Wingan Inlet and the heart of Croajingolong.*
P71: *The Koala survives in Australia's national parks and reserves but is threatened elsewhere by loss of habitat.*

Currawong. At sunrise and sunset, range upon range of diminishing blue or smoking gold extends to the horizon.

Magnificent Landcapes

The wonderful and varied landscapes of this park are the result of the area's tortured geomorphology. Millions of years ago, as the Victorian Alps were born, great creases tore at the land crunching and cracking it in a series of faults, some of which allowed lava to escape from the depths to flow across parts of the crumpled surface.

A number of these deep rips or faults were eroded to become the Alpine National Park's mighty Wonnangatta, Wongungarra, Kiewa and Macalister river valleys, covered today with tall forests broken by grasslands. The flat-topped Mount Jim and Mount Loch and the rich Wellington Plains – 'parkland' covered with scattered stands of picturesque Snow Gums amongst grassy plains – are the basaltic remains of ancient lava flows.

To the north, great blisters of tough granite have been exposed to form Mount Buffalo and Mount Bogong, popular winter snowfields. Aboriginal people living far from the mountains once made an annual pilgrimage to the Bogong High Plains to together feast for days on nutritious roasted Bogong moths, collecting them from beneath the boulders of the high tops where they gathered in their tens of thousands.

Elsewhere in the park, vast masses of ancient slates and sedimentary rocks have been folded and eroded into a number of sharp razorback ridges including Mount Feathertop (spectacular when snow-covered), The Viking (so-called because its rising fold resembles the bows of a mighty longship), The Razor and the ridges around Mount Hotham and The Bluff.

Location: Extends across the eastern 200 km (124 miles) of the Victorian section of the Great Dividing Range and peripheral alpine and subalpine ranges contiguous with Kosciuszko National Park.

Climate: Extreme; winter and spring snows lie for 4–6 months on heights, lighter snow and many frosts elsewhere. Short summer can reach 35° C (95° F) from December to March. Weather extremely changeable. Extreme care needed in marginal periods.

When to Go: Winter sports, June–September. Wildflowers, October–January; car touring, November–April. Bushwalking, November–May.

Access: By car, 3–5 hour drive from Melbourne; main access via Omeo, Bright, Mansfield, Dargo and Licola. By air to Dinner Plain airfield. 4WD road closures over winter begin June 1, end October 31. Check detail at visitor centres.

Permits: None required.

Equipment: Cars in winter must carry snow chains. Bushwalking and camping gear, strong shoes or boots, warm clothing and wet weather gear, ski equipment, first-aid kit, SPF 30+ sunscreen, hat, trout-fishing gear, fuel stove and fuel, binoculars, large-scale maps.

Facilities: Visitor information centres at Bright, Mt Beauty, Bairnsdale, Mansfield and Omeo; ski resorts at Mt Hotham, Falls Creek, Dinner Plain, Mt Buller, Mt Buffalo. 4WD tracks and picnic areas. Camping areas with facilities, full accommodation at nearby towns.

Watching Wildlife: Special features include Gang Gang Cockatoos, Peregrine Falcons, Grey Kangaroos, wombats, Swamp Wallabies, echidnas, Platypus, Brushtail Possums, gliders and Lyrebirds in forests.

Visitor Activities: Walking, car touring (2WD and 4WD), nature study, trout fishing, canoeing.

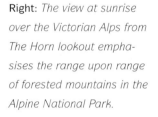

Above: *The male Superb Lyrebird,* Menura novaehollandiae, *is a spectacular mimic – it sings and dances for its hen, displaying fabulous tail feathers.*

Right: *The view at sunrise over the Victorian Alps from The Horn lookout emphasises the range upon range of forested mountains in the Alpine National Park.*

above, rocky ridges with masses of boulders shelter the elusive Mountain Pygmy Possum. Thought to have been extinct for thousands of years, this possum was recently rediscovered in a ridgetop stockman's hut in the park. These high areas are snow-covered for four to six months each year, during which time most animals lie in torpor or live in insulated undersnow tunnels and nests.

Snowgrass Summits

A spectacular mix of plant communities covers any of the summits near Mount Hotham, the piled up granite Horn on Mount Buffalo, Falls Creek or Mount Howitt – all areas easily accessible via the park's network of 2WD and 4WD roads and walking tracks. At the highest levels, snowgrass cover mixes with herbfields rich in spring and early summer flowers, many daisy species being most prevalent.

The high broad valleys have more shrub cover, although cattle are still grazed in many areas. Remnant bogs, pitifully reduced after a century of grazing, and sphagnum lie in the wet centres of these valleys while, high

Below the Treeline

Just below the treeline, Snow Gum and Black Sally woodlands are broken by herbfield and shrubland valley bottoms and clear frost hollows. Wet Black Sally limbs shine like highly buffed bronze in the sunlight while Snow Gums (White Sallys) are beautifully streaked and sculpted by the environment. The floor here is dominated by snowgrass peppered with bright pink Trigger Plants, yellow daisies, pale mauve Eye Brights and Alpine Mint – countless halcyon campsites beckon the bushwalker.

Below the Snow Gums, tree height increases until Mountain Gums give way to the tallest montane forests dominated by towering Alpine Ash. The smooth silvery trunks of these magnificent trees rise from a rough-barked base for 60 metres (197 feet) or more. This forest type cuts out dramatically at an altitude of around 1,100 metres (3,608 feet) to be replaced by mixed eucalypt forest.

CROAJINGOLONG NATIONAL PARK

Wilderness Coast

Established in 1979, Croajingolong National Park today differs little from the coast Captain James Cook, an early European explorer, observed in 1770 after sailing east from New Zealand. It was then and is now 'rather low and not very hilly, the face of the country is green and woody but the sea shore is all white sand.' Low undulating shaly ridges rise inland from the sandy coast to Howe Hill (391 metres/1,282 feet) and Genoa Peak (489 metres/1,604 feet) – the highest points in the park. These granite intrusions are the landlocked versions of Gabo Island and The Skerries, just offshore.

Cook also noted the presence of 'lawns' – extensive coastal heathlands backed by heavy forest – but missed the large tranquil lagoons hidden behind beach dune barriers at Tamboon, Thurra River, Mueller Inlet, Wingan and Mallacoota.

Today's park is 875 square kilometres (338 square miles) in area and stretches west along the Victorian coast for 95 kilometres (59 miles) from the New South Wales border at Cape Howe to Sydenham Inlet. The lake system that forms Mallacoota Inlet is the only place where civilization comes to Croajingolong. Most of this wild area is so little changed from Cook's time – Croajingolong shelters over 1,000 plant species and 300 bird species – that it was listed in the first group of Australia's World Biosphere reserves in 1977.

'Green and Woody'

Cook's green and woody ridges are covered by tall dry sclerophyll forest of Coastal Ash, Yellow Stringybark and

Above right: Native Fuchsia, Correa reflexa, *is found in the coastal heathlands of Croajingolong National Park.*

White Stringybark eucalypts with an understorey of acacias, Geebungs, Kunzea, Pink Heath, grasses and aromatic Daisy Bush – the territory of the Grey Forester Kangaroo.

The drive into Wingan Inlet is typical of the roads into this elongated park. Leaving the Princes Highway, the road slips down the coastal slopes into a world of damp gullies where ferns increase and the mix of eucalypts becomes more luxuriant. Here, the understorey is wild and lush with lacy tree ferns and King Ferns, tangled runners of thorny Lawyer Vine, Saw Sedge, Weeping Tea Tree, Blackwood, and Pittosporum. These damp forests ring with the clear mimicking calls of the Lyrebird and the steady tinkling of Bell Birds.

Ringtail possums, shy Swamp Wallabies and Wombats are typical inhabitants of these forests. At night, Yellow-bellied Gliders, Greater Gliders and Sugar Gliders are prey to the Powerful Owl. However, most wildlife in Australia is nocturnal and cryptic, and the best time to view bushland mammals is either very early in the morning or late in the day. This is easy to achieve when bush-camping in the wilderness zone or somewhere along the Coast Track.

Marshes and Heathlands

A mosaic of marshes dominated by Saw Sedge spreads across the depressions close to the sea and around the estuaries and coast. Tea Trees and paperbarks, with their powdery parchment layers of soft creamy bark, line the waterways. Open woodlands of magnificent Rough Barked Angophoras, twisted 'Old Man' banksias and Bloodwood eucalypts cover the hind dune areas where the car campsites are located. Beneath the trees, tall heath plants such as Grasstrees, scented Pink Boronia

Location: Far eastern coast of Victoria between Cape Howe and Bemm River; 450 km (279 miles) east of Melbourne and 550 km (342 miles) south of Sydney.

Climate: Warm summers, some hot days with special fire restrictions; cool winters with a number of wet days. Some frosts inland.

When to Go: Anytime. Best for flowers, August–November; best for canoeing, walking and swimming, August–April.

Access: By sealed road from Hwy 1 to Mallacoota, then gravel road into the park. Various unsealed roads (often impassable in wet weather) from Hwy 1 to different coastal areas of the park. By air from Mallacoota or Merimbula to Gabo Island. Jetty on Gabo Island.

Permits: Camping permit from parks office, Cann River. Bookings necessary for lighthouse accommodation on Gabo Island and at Point Hicks.

Equipment: Camping gear, water bottle, cool-weather clothes, showerproof wind jacket, strong walking shoes/boots, sandshoes, swimming gear, hat, raincoat, insect repellent (mosquitoes and ticks), first-aid kit, sunscreen SPF 30+; binoculars; strong torch for night spotting.

Facilities: Camping areas, marked coastal walking track, picnic areas, water provided, self-guided nature walks. Visitor information centres at Cann River and Mallacoota, lighthouse accommodation at Point Hicks and Gabo Island.

Watching Wildlife: Most mammals ubiquitous, spotlighting for small mammals, phalangers and possums on dark nights. Honeyeaters, August–November; Lyrebirds, June–September; Mutton Birds (Wedgetailed Shearwaters), mid–October and April. Fur Seals and Sea Lions along coast and on the Skerries.

Visitor Activities: Wildflower study, swimming, walking, canoeing, sailing, fishing, sea kayaking.

Right: *Point Hicks is close to the first spot European explorer Captain James Cook saw when he came upon Australia after sailing west from New Zealand.*

Below: *Powerful Owls are easily the largest of the Australian owls (this one is immature), with a secure population in the wilderness of Croajingolong.*

and Golden Glory Peas grow along with a host of other plants on the warm sandy floor. The boardwalk track which skirts the Wingan Inlet is one of the best places in the park to experience this type of habitat.

On exposed seaward slopes the 'lawns' begin. Heath plants emerge from the forest to become a solid knee-high to waist-deep mass of colourful spring flowers. Several species of bonsai-form banksias, hakeas, acacias and mallee-form Bloodwoods grow in thickets which shelter Grey Kangaroos and the odd Diamond Python. These perfumed heathlands, which continue into the New South Wales Nadgee Nature Reserve and Ben Boyd National Park, are a mecca for honeyeaters

and the last major refuge for the endangered Ground Parrot. This greenish bird with yellow and lime-green barred feathers nests on the floor of the heath. It was nearly extinct after being hunted for food across the rest of its heathland range by early settlers who also cleared and burned its habitat to run cattle.

Beaches and Lagoons

About 14,000 years ago, when the sea began drowning this coast, the local Krauetungulung and Bidawal Aboriginal people were driven from their campsites along the shore. Over many generations, the communities moved inland ahead of the sea until, around 6,000

Above: *The flower-laden Crimson Bottlebrush, Callistemon sp., is a rich nectar-producer on the fringes of Croajingolong's coastal wetlands.*

Left: *The Thurra Swamp wetlands and open waters create fine habitat for the park's Black Swans and other waterbirds.*

years ago, sea levels stabilised. The drift of sand across the bay mouths cut many inlets off from the sea creating the tranquil lagoons of today's national park. These quiet waters, all of which break through to the sea from time to time, are important nurseries for fish such as Mullet, Bream, Flathead, Whiting and Bass.

Ancient stories and songs passed down through the generations to today's Bidawal and Krauetungulung people tell of the great retreat. These proud local Aboriginal people suffered greatly after first European contact, but the Victorian government is beginning to realise how effective joint management of parks by traditional owners and park staff has been in other States.

Mutton Birds in the Sunrise

Around the middle of October, lucky campers anywhere along this coast within sight of the sea will witness a remarkable and beautiful phenomenon. Sunrise over the water is always a brilliant spectacle but, at this time of year, as the light slowly brightens, a grey patchy mass moving south just above the opalescent water draws the eye. Millions of Short-tailed Shearwaters, almost at the end of a trans-Pacific flight to their nesting areas by Bass Strait, fly just above the swells in vast flocks. Moving like clockwork, the stream unbroken for two days, these birds are geared to a mysterious cycle that will see egg-laying commencing between 19 and 21 November exactly.

WILSONS PROMONTORY NATIONAL PARK

Southernmost Mainland Australia

Just 200 kilometres (124 miles) south-east of Melbourne, Victoria's capital city, Wilsons Promontory National Park (the 'Prom') is a favourite weekend and day visit area. Sandy bays and coves punctuate the rocky shoreline, with 40 kilometres of high granite ranges forming a spectacular backdrop to the coastal scenery. Tall eucalypt forests, heathlands and salt marshes are found inland, and well-marked tracks allow for easy exploration near the main campground of Tidal River. To the north the Prom becomes wilder, with no facilities and limited fresh water – a remote yet beautiful area visited by experienced bushwalkers.

As recently as 12,000 years ago this southernmost point of mainland Australia was the beginning of a land-bridge linking Tasmania with the mainland. The small island that remained after the seas rose and drowned the land-bridge was gradually connected to the mainland again by a narrow spit of sand. In 1798 George Bass was the first European to see this 'lofty, hummocky promontory of hard granite', and exactly 100 years later the area became Victoria's second national park.

The park today is 503 square kilometres (194 square miles) in area and encompasses the entire peninsula south of Forster on the Yanakie isthmus – the sandy neck connecting Wilsons Promontory to the mainland at

Opposite: *Late afternoon light transforms Norman Bay, on the west coast of Wilsons Promontory, into liquid gold.*

Above right: *The Azure Kingfisher,* Alcedo azurea, *can sometimes be spotted fishing in the park's mountain pools.*

Corner Inlet. Ten small rocky islands just offshore are also part of the park, and a number of adjacent marine reservations comprising a total of 280 square kilometres (108 square miles) were proclaimed in 1986. In 1982 Wilsons Promontory was listed as a World Biosphere Reserve because of the richness of its living systems. At the same time, 505 square kilometres (195 square miles) of peripheral wetlands at Corner Inlet were listed as Wetlands of International Importance under the RAMSAR Convention.

Fens to Forest

Over many thousands of years the broad bay created by the Yanakie isthmus has slowly filled with sediment and wind-blown sand. Today, a series of vast sandy shallows and mudflats support a succession of sea-grass and mangrove marine nurseries. Moving away from the water, fleshy leaved samphire near the shoreline merges into wet heathlands, which soon give way to Banksia and Tea Tree scrub rising to frontal dune vegetation – all important bird habitats. Migratory waders such as Whimbrels, Snipes, Mongolian Sand Plovers, Tattlers, Stints and Godwits over-summer on the flats, while massive numbers of Australian honeyeaters flock to the flowering heaths.

Much of the indigenous life in the mountainous areas of the park is linked with Tasmania – a result of the early land bridge. So in the high south-facing and protected gully aspects there are tall creamy-trunked Mountain Ash, Messmate and Blue Gum forests rising above tree ferns and cool rainforest thickets of Myrtle Beech, Lilly Pilly and Blackwood. Altogether there are about 750 plant species in the mosaic of communities in the park.

Location: The most southern point of the Australian mainland, 200 km (124 miles) south-east of Melbourne, the State capital.

Climate: Average maximum temperatures range from 12° C (54° F) in winter to 21° C (70° F) in summer. Average of 19 raindays in July, 9 in January; annual average rainfall is 1,050 mm (42 inches). Frequent strong westerly winds.

When to Go: The climate is most comfortable from September–April. The park is extremely busy in September, December and January. Wildflowers are at their peak from August–October.

Access: By road from Melbourne to Foster and Tidal River via the South Gippsland Highway or the Princes Highway.

Permits: Park entry permit and camping permits from park headquarters and entry station. Bookings for accommodation essential.

Equipment: Camping gear, hat, sunscreen, insect repellent, rain gear, warm clothing and wind jacket, strong walking shoes able to cope with wet conditions, swimming gear, snorkelling gear, binoculars.

Facilities: Campground with all facilities available at Tidal River, backpack campsites at 11 locations, visitor information centre at Tidal River; ranger service; self-guided trails; over 100 km (62 miles) of walking tracks throughout the park. Popular cabin, unit, hut, lodge and lighthouse accommodation all available within the park, all require booking well in advance.

Watching Wildlife: Relatively tame parrots and wallabies, numerous opportunistic sightings. Migratory waders October–April, other waterbirds, including numerous swans, can be seen on Corner Inlet.

Visitor Activities: Picnicking, swimming and snorkelling, marine and shoreline study, birdwatching, wildflower and plant study, walking.

Map labels: Mt Margaret; Melbourne; Millers Landing; Rabbit Island; Wilsons Promontory National Park; Five Mile Beach; Shellback Island; Sparkes Lookout; Norman Island; Tidal River; Glennie Group; N; Anser Group; Lighthouse; South East Point

Lyrebirds, Yellow Robins and Wonga Pigeons are among the birds that can be spotted in the more mountainous areas. In fact, around 180 species of birds from Little Penguins to magnificent White-bellied Sea Eagles — more than a third of all bird species found in Victoria — are found in the park. Swamp Wallabies and Ringtail Possums are also heard and seen in the damp gullies. Even the usually difficult-to-find Koalas can sometimes be spotted sleeping in the Blue Gums.

Sealers Lead the Charge

The drier woodlands and heathy areas on the lower slopes and ridges of the park are punctuated here and

Left: *Lucky visitors may spot one of the park's Koalas,* Phascolarctos cinereus, *high in the canopy of a Blue Gum.*

there with beautiful grey, lichen-encrusted granite tors and occasional reminders of the past — a rusty ring, a piece of chain or wire. George Bass' report on his voyage of discovery described large numbers of fur seals on the islands and shorelines of the strait, and sealers and whalers soon made their way to the area.

Some of the place names also recall the past lives of the promontory. Sheltered Sealers Cove is squeezed between the eastern slopes of the promontory's highest mountain, Mount Latrobe (754 metres/2,473 feet), and Mount Wilson (705 metres/2,312 feet). The cove has a delightful beach and is on the route of one of the park's most popular overnight walks — the Sealers Cove–Refuge Cove–Waterloo Bay track.

The track runs for 36 kilometres (22 miles) across the southern end of the park and takes at least several days

to complete. Tin Mine Cove is another reminder of Wilsons Promontory's working past, when mining, timber getting and grazing were important in the area.

Some of the buildings in the park are also legacies of pre-park activities on the 'Prom'. During World War II, Tidal River was a base for commando training and for many years the promontory was home to a series of lighthouse keepers. The main park campground and accommodation has grown around the original army barracks area and, perched far out on the smoothly rounded granite hump of South East Cape, the lighthouse (now automated) and associated cottages, built in 1859, are used as park accommodation.

Active on the 'Prom'

There are over 100 kilometres (60 miles) of walking tracks in the park ranging from short self-guided nature trails to overnight walks such as the one to South Point, mainland Australia's most southerly point. The walks vary in difficulty although most are relatively easy and many include large sections of boardwalk. Walks start either from park headquarters at Tidal River or, for walks into the northern areas of the park, at the Miller Landing carpark. With 130 kilometres (81 miles) of coastline, the park also offers plenty of opportunities for swimming, although the water can be chilly. Whatever the activity, it is important to remember that weather changes come in rapid succession at Wilsons Promontory.

Overleaf: *Lilly Pilly Gully, with its treeferns and cool temperate rainforest relicts, is habitat for many marsupials.*

Above: *White sand and granite boulders line the estuary at the south end of Five Mile Beach.*

Below: *Eastern Grey Kangaroos graze on old farmland within the park.*

PORT CAMPBELL NATIONAL PARK

The Spectacular 'Shipwreck Coast'

Port Campbell National Park stretches in a narrow band for 43 kilometres (27 miles) along the southern coastline of Victoria from Peterborough, 53 kilometres (33 miles) east of Warrnambool, to Princetown. Proclaimed in 1965, the park encompasses much of the so-called 'Shipwreck Coast', with dozens of known wrecks dotting the waters below the cliffs. While small in area – 17.5 square kilometres (6.7 square miles) – the park protects one of the most magnificent coastlines in Australia. Brilliant ochre and pale yellow vertical limestone cliffs have been eaten away by the powerful seas of the Southern Ocean to form the area's famous sea stacks as well as spectacular gorges, blowholes and beaches. The journey to Port Campbell along the scenic Great Ocean Road from Melbourne, 250 kilometres to the east, is almost as delightful as the park itself.

Sculptures by the Sea

The Port Campbell coast is a young coast, its beds of limestone comprising a mix of granular calcium carbonate and masses of seashell pieces and skeletons of marine organisms deposited on a warm shallow ocean bed about 20 million years ago. As sea levels rose and opened Bass Strait, the prevailing westerly swell began to batter the soft limestone shoreline. Huge gutters were cut running inland to the north-east, aided by a trend in that direction of the joints and by a softer

Opposite: *Southern Ocean Waves crashing on soft limestone has produced Victoria's remarkable 'Shipwreck Coast'.*

Above right: *The Little or Fairy Penguin,* Eudyptula minor, *nests in tunnels around the southern coast of Australia.*

lower bed. At the heads of many gutters, tunnels have formed through the softer rock and the explosive pressure of the air trapped by massive waves has blasted very impressive blowholes up to the surface. One tunnel runs for a hundred metres before erupting through a huge hole 40 metres (131 feet) in diameter, 17 metres deep (56 feet) and still growing.

Bridges and Stacks

Ultimately the cave or tunnel roof collapses and the gorge moves further inland. Many of these mighty parallel gutters join as their separating walls are undercut – first forming bridges, then, as these collapse, an island is isolated. This happened in spectacular fashion in 1990 when part of 'London Bridge' became an island with one sudden rumble. Stranded tourists were rescued unharmed from the remaining section. These stocky islands are, in turn, undercut and a combination of sea spray, wind and rain sculpt them into the towering sea stack forms of the Twelve Apostles. Like the original Apostles, of which eight remain, all sea stacks will die, crumbling into the sea to become grains of sand on nearby beaches. The limestone stretches far inland, however, and new gutters, tunnels, bridges, islands and stacks will continue to form for many thousands of years to come.

The Loch Ard Disaster

Nobody knows why the *Loch Ard*, a clipper ship, was sailing close inshore during wild winter weather in 1878. When the ship ran aground near a deep opening in the cliffs, since named the Loch Ard Gorge, it became part of the tragic history of the 'Shipwreck Coast'. Midshipman Tom Pearce survived by holding onto a lifeline then

Location: 250 km (155 miles) south-west of Melbourne stretching in a thin strip along the coast west of Cape Otway between Princetown and Peterborough.

Climate: Winter is cool, windy and wet; summer is warm with some hot days. The area can experience rapid weather changes in the spring and in summer.

When to Go: Best in the spring and through summer and autumn. Spring wildflower display. Grand ocean display during winter storms.

Access: By car via the dramatic Great Ocean Road, 3–4 hours from Melbourne or 45 minutes from Warrnambool.

Permits: No permits are required as there is no camping in the park.

Equipment: Warm clothing, showerproof jacket, comfortable shoes, binoculars for close inspection of sea stacks and for birdwatching (seabirds in the park include Wedge-tailed Shearwaters, also known as Muttonbirds, and Little Penguins), sunscreen.

Facilities: Strategic clifftop carparks, clifftop walkway, steps to beaches. Self-guided nature discovery walk. Visitor information centre, accommodation and a camping/caravan park available in Port Campbell township.

Watching Wildlife: Honeyeaters are easily spotted on the springtime flowering heath behind the cliffs. Numerous seabirds, including many Northern Hemisphere migratory species, can be seen nesting and resting on the cliffs and stacks from September–April.

Visitor Activities: Scenic drives, walking, birdwatching, swimming, surfing, snorkelling on calm days.

Above: *London Bridge was once double-arched and joined to the mainland.*

Right: *Visitors view the Twelve Apostles from a platform by the roadside.*

Opposite: *These limestone stacks are the so-called Twelve Apostles, but their numbers are gradually being eroded by the sea.*

swimming to the beach at the head of the gorge. He found spirits and food washed up from the boat and was making a meal when he was interrupted by screaming. He saw Eva Carmichael clinging to wreckage, swam out and, gripping her clothing in his teeth, dragged her to safety and revived her by rubbing her body with brandy. He then climbed the cliff and sought help from farmers at 'Glenample' homestead. Pearce and Carmichael were the only survivors of 47 passengers and crew. Today,

visitors to the park can explore historic 'Glenample' and climb down the steep gorge stairway to the picturesque beach where Eva Carmichael was rescued.

From the Loch Ard Gorge follow the Historic Shipwreck Trail – each wreck is marked with an information plaque – to Peterborough. Along the way, stop off at Port Campbell where the Loch Ard Shipwreck Museum tells the stories of the wrecks along the coast and displays artefacts salvaged from some of the disasters.

A Rich Natural History

Most visitors come to Port Campbell National Park for the grandeur of the coast – sea stacks wreathed in the golden vapours of wild waves at sunset, a Masefield 'grey dawn breaking', the bright colours and breaking seas of a fine day. But, in springtime, brilliant wildflowers cover the coastal heath creating a blaze of colour of their own. With the flowers come the honeyeaters, although birdwatchers in the park are usually found gazing out to sea from the many clifftop lookouts and walkways. From September to April, Shearwaters in their thousands sweep the waters, returning to the stacks and islands – particularly Mutton Bird Island – every evening. Rafts of Little (Fairy) Penguins are also regularly seen and heard.

GRAMPIANS NATIONAL PARK

The Noble Ranges

The Grampians National Park, also known by the Aboriginal name 'Gariwerd' lies across the tail end of Australia's Great Dividing Range, 258 kilometres (160 miles) along the Western Highway from Melbourne. Established in 1984, this national park protects 1,672 square kilometres (645 square miles) of rugged country, waterfalls and lakes amidst an ocean of agricultural land.

Three great parallel curving ranges of sandstone, extending 95 kilometres (59 miles) north to south and 55 kilometres (34 miles) east to west, rise abruptly from the flat expanse of the surrounding countryside. The eastern or front range is named after its highest peak, Mount William (1,167 metres/3,828 feet). The combined Serra and Mount Difficult ranges in the middle are separated from Mount William Range by Fyans Creek and Wannon River and from the back Victoria Range by the Glenelg River.

A Mountainous Reservoir

Set aside as a State forest in 1872, this area was worked for timber, quarry stone and minerals but most importantly it served, and continues to serve, as the domestic and stock water supply area for western Victoria. The park protects the catchments of 12 reservoirs and lakes, with the headwaters of the streams on the ranges receiving between 750 and 1000 mm (30–40 inches) of rain during a large number of rain days each year.

The high local rainfall has etched out amazing rock formations including Whales Mouth, Nerve Test, Fallen Giant, Jaws of Death and Wonderland – echoes of a time when a visit to The Grampians was considered the height of adventure. Today, the park offers over 50 bushwalks along marked tracks and many kilometres of roads, sealed and 4WD. Small towns dot the surrounding farmland and the drive from Melbourne takes just a few hours.

A Thousand Wildflowers

Broken sandstone mountain country, because of its many micro-habitats, generally has a rich flora, and The Grampians are no exception. Over a thousand species, one third of Victoria's flora, have been identified amongst the park's varied plant communities. High cold tops support a stunted woodland and heathland while cliff terraces and rocky pockets form islands of individual plant mixes. Woodland-covered slopes and forested, fern-filled gullies and valley floors lie waiting to be explored. Wetter habitats include extensive areas of hanging and bottomland swamp as well as permanent streams and waterfall seepage areas and stillwater pondages.

From August to December a series of flowering peaks occurs. First comes the gold of the wattles, splashed with the stunning purple and green of the climber False Sarsaparilla, and the rich pinks of Common Heath (the State emblem) and Grampians Heath. Tiny furred White Beards mingle with red Native Fuchsias and grevilleas.

Opposite: These sandstone 'balconies' on the Serra Range in the Grampians are sometimes called the 'Jaws of Death'.

Above right: Peregrine Falcons, Falco peregrinus, nest on Grampian cliff ledges and prey on smaller birds flying below.

Grampians National Park map showing: To Horsham, Mt Zero, Mt Difficult, Wartook Reservoir, Stawell, Halls Gap, N, Mt Thackeray, Mt Frederick, Grampians National Park, Moyston, To Ararat, Victoria Piont, To Hamilton, Melbourne, Dunkeld

Above: *Mt Abrupt, a classic sandstone cuesta tableland, is typical of the way the Grampians rise from surrounding country.*

Above: *One glance at the flower of a Duck Orchid, Caleana major, and its name needs no explanation.*

Scented and Climbing Sundews and the exquisite blue Viola flourish in the wet places. Soon spring and early summer sets the mountains afire in unbelievable colour, bringing the honey flow and the birds!

The Cunning Orchids

Beneath the ferns, among the mosses, sprouting from the rich damp mulch of the forest and woodland floor – or even the sheltered floor of the dry heath – the most exquisite and 'cunning' plants of all show themselves at irregular intervals. Geared to specific changes in the environment, most of the 80 or so species of ground orchids are triggered to flower by a temperature change or a change in nutrients. Some are even stimulated by gases in bushfire smoke or the chemicals released from ashes.

After flowering, some orchids ensure pollination with their brilliant colours, others have built-in avenues and traffic lines marking the way in. The Mosquito Orchids provide tiny insect landing grounds and the Musky Caladenia imitates insect sex pheromones causing the insect to attempt to mate with the orchid. The exquisite Duck Orchid locks out nectar and pollen thieves when its 'approved' pollinating agent is not around.

A Place of Sanctuary

The varied habitats of The Grampians are a sanctuary for terrestrial, arboreal, aquatic and bird life – an oasis in the middle of the vast areas of western Victoria cleared for sheep and cattle grazing and for wheat production. The park shelters 31 species of native mammals, over 200 bird species, 31 reptile, 11 amphibian and seven fish species as well as many invertebrates.

The labrador-sized Brush-tailed Rock-wallaby, thought to be almost extinct in Victoria, has now been found in several small colonies on cliff terraces in The Grampians. The Heath Rat is another special case – a gentle native rodent found only in the Grampians and in small colonies in south-west Victoria. For successful over-wintering and breeding, this animal requires a variety of heath plant food that develops only in the period of six to nine years after fire – an unusual requirement, which raises a crucial park management issue.

The First People

In 1836, when Surveyor General Thomas Mitchell named these mountains after the Grampians of the Scottish Highlands, it is believed that up to 4,000

Above: *The roof shape of the Brambuk Aboriginal Cultural Centre at Halls Gap represents the curves of an Aboriginal bark shelter.*

Above left: *Eastern grey Kangaroos,* Macropus giganteus, *are at the edge of their range in the Grampians National Park.*

Left: *Laughing Kookaburras,* Dacelo novaeguineae, *are carnivores that often become too friendly as they loiter about campsites waiting for a handout.*

Aboriginal people belonging to three different language groups inhabited the area, living on the very rich plant and animal resources available, including fish.

The plentiful supply of food and the consequent stability of the local Aboriginal people – there were regular ceremonial gatherings of 1,000 or more people – might explain the many fine examples of rock art in the park. Paintings are usually found on the sandstone walls of the rock shelters near where the people camped. While some of these shelters are open to the public, many more are off-limits, although tours can be organized from Brambuk Aboriginal cultural centre at Halls Gap.

TASMANIA

Tasmania, 'the island State', is the smallest of Australia's eight States and Territories, comprising just 0.9 per cent of the land. A total area of 68,049 square kilometres (26,267 square miles) includes the main shield-shaped island, lying off the south-eastern tip of the mainland, as well as several much smaller islands. Tasmania's coastline is 3,200 kilometres (1,987 miles) long and embraces fiords, large bays, magnificent beaches — such as those at Freycinet National Park halfway up the east coast — and some of the most dramatic seacliffs in Australia.

As in continental Australia, the State's largest cities and towns are on the coast. Unlike the mainland, Tasmania is a well-watered place with no large seasonal concentrations of rain. The main island extends from latitude 40°38' S to 43°39' S, facing the rain-bearing Roaring Forties of the Southern Ocean, which bring the west coast and highlands over 3,000 mm (120 inches) of rain per year. The east remains in rainshadow, protected from the Roaring Forties by the State's rugged mountains.

At least half of Tasmania — including the Central Highlands and the remote south-west — is dominated by wet heath-covered high mountains and dramatic peaks, many rising above shallow tarns and picturesque lakes scraped from the landscape by long-dead glaciers. The highest is Mount Ossa at 1,617 metres (5,304 feet). Wide areas of fen, bog, swamp and moor, many covered for weeks in winter snow, merge into primeval, moss-floored Myrtle Beech forests. Downslope, towering eucalypt forests grow on deep damp soils. To the east and north of the highlands the lower more fertile wooded lands have been cleared for farming.

Mount Field National Park, just west of Hobart, the State capital, shelters the most accessible of the glaciated landscapes, although walkers from around the world are drawn to the spectacular multi-day Overland Track of Cradle Mountain–Lake St Clair National Park in the north-west. South of Lake St Clair, the wild, wet mountainscapes of the spectacular Southwest and the Franklin–Gordon Wild Rivers national parks became world-famous in the 1970s when a dramatic environmental battle prevented a second dam on the Gordon River.

FREYCINET NATIONAL PARK

Tasmania's Côte d'Azur

Halfway up the east coast of Tasmania lies a long and mountainous pink granite peninsula, much of which is protected within Freycinet National Park. Just 200 kilometres (124 miles) by road north-east of Hobart, the park was established in 1916 and named after Louis Claude de Saulces de Freycinet, cartographer of the first major scientific expedition to Australia (1800–1804).

Extending south in a narrow strip along the coast from just below Bicheno on the ocean side of the peninsula, the park gradually widens until it encompasses the entire peninsula south of Coles Bay. Schouten Island, the large island off the peninsula's southern tip, was added in 1967, bringing the total park area to 119 square kilometres (46 square miles).

Freycinet is dominated by two parallel mountain ranges of which the highest peak is Mount Freycinet at 620 metres (2,034 feet). These wooded and scrub-covered ranges – The Hazards to the north and the Freycinet group to the south – are separated by a wide sandy isthmus. Two lines of wind-built beach frontal dunes on either side of the isthmus are separated by a major wetland area with a number of lagoons highly attractive to birdlife.

Opposite: *Wineglass Bay spreads out below the Mt Amos lookout, with Mt Freycinet in the background at the right.*

Above right: *Black Swans,* Cygnus atratus, *are common on the park lagoons and on Great Oyster Bay to the west.*

Previous pages

P92: *Ancient glaciated landscapes at Schnells Ridge, Mt Anne area, Southwest NP and Tasmanian Wilderness WHA.*
P93: *The Common Wombat is found in all Tasmanian parks.*

Map labels: Hobart; Great Oyster Bay; Coles Bay (Park HQ); Mt Amos; Wineglass Bay; Freycinet National Park; Freycinet Peninsula; N; Schouten Island

Tasmania's Côte d'Azur

The shoreline of Freycinet is strung with glorious beaches set against the sometimes wild and grey but mostly flawless azure of the surrounding waters. Dozens of bewitching coves and inlets shelter beaches of spectacular boulders and white sand. Even the larger beaches facing west are special. A limpid lagoon behind Bryans Beach is a fine place to catch Southern Bream. Hazards Beach, backed by giant dunes, stretches for two kilometres along Great Oyster Bay on the western side of the isthmus. On the other side, a breathtaking curve of white beach lines the shore of glorious Wineglass Bay.

Tracking the Landscape

The climb up Mount Amos or the four-hour loop walk around Mount Mayson are both good introductions to the area. Wineglass Bay self-guided nature track leaves the coastal she-oaks and woodland and climbs through pockets of scrub and heath past towering granite tors to the saddle between mounts Amos and Mayson. The Mount Amos lookout further up, surrounded by gigantic pink tors, offers a birds-eye view of the azure waters of Wineglass Bay backed by a mosaic of greens around the wetland ponds of the isthmus and, beyond, Great Oyster Bay.

From the saddle the track drops quickly to the sandy isthmus and an overnight campsite. Bennett's Wallabies can usually be spotted during a sunrise wander around the camp, and an Eastern Quoll, Brushtail Possum, Swamp Rat or Water Rat may be seen near the lagoon.

Location: Spreads across the Freycinet Peninsula 200 km (124 miles) north-east of Hobart, halfway up the east coast of Tasmania.

Climate: Cool, damp winters with south-westerly and southerly winds. Warm, dry summers with rapid weather changes; hot, windy afternoons. Periods of fire danger.

When to Go: Anytime from August–April, although the clikmate is most comfortable during warmer months from November–February.

Access: By road via the Tasman Hwy to Coles Bay, Parsons Cove, Cape Tourville. Boat from Swansea, Little Swanport and Coles Bay.

Permits: Camping permits available from national parks ranger and information office at Coles Bay, bookings are advisable for campsites, especially in school holidays. Fire restrictions apply.

Equipment: Camping gear, water, fuel stove and fuel, warm clothes, swimming gear, fishing gear, hat, sunscreen, strong boots for hill walks, otherwise sandshoes, camera with macro and 35–125 mm lenses and binoculars.

Facilities: Major camping and caravan area at Coles Bay, also general store. Barbecues and toilets at Honeymoon Bay and Rangers Creek. Backpack campsites at Hazards Beach, Cooks Beach, Bryans Beach and Wineglass Bay all with pit toilets, limited water supply. Walking tracks into park from main centres. Ranger services.

Watching Wildlife: Wallabies and possums can be seen around campsites. Waterbirds and seabirds can be seen in the park including large populations of Black Swans. Wildflowers are at their best from August–December.

Visitor Activities: Boating, fishing, walking, nature study, birdwatching, swimming, rock climbing.

Above: *Crimson Rosellas are found throughout Tasmania's woodlands and eucalypt forests.*

Top: *Mt Amos, with its rounded granite faces and heath and woodland cover, is typical of Freycinet NP.*

Far right: *Bennett's Wallaby is often seen near the park's walking tracks.*

Skirting the northern end of the isthmus, the track passes close to a lagoon usually dotted with Black Ducks, Grey Teal, Black Swans and the flightless Native Hens; about 150 bird species have been recorded in the park. Any of Tasmania's three species of snake – the Island Tiger Snake, Copperhead or the White-lipped Whipsnake – might be spotted near the lagoon. All are venomous.

From Hazards Beach on Great Oyster Bay, the loop returns via the main Peninsula Track. Along this part of the track, Aboriginal middens – the heaped remains of mostly seafood feasts accumulated over the past 6,000 years – can be seen in parts of the blown-out dunes.

Dry Side of Tasmania

By the time rain-bearing winds reach Freycinet, much of the moisture has precipitated on the highlands further west. Although over a third of Tasmania's plant species can be found in Freycinet, vegetation in the park and along the coast to the north, once connected to the mainland, is more like the Gippsland coast of eastern Victoria than anywhere else in Tasmania.

To the south, a 26-kilometre (16-mile) circuit track cuts through tough fire-hardened scrub to Mount Freycinet and Bryans Beach – bushfire is one of the hazards of living in rainshadow. The heathlands along this track between Cooks Corner and Bryans are particularly rich in wildflowers including Pink Heath, Fringed Myrtle,

Wild Iris, hakeas and numerous orchids including the Wax-lip, Spider, Spotted Sun, Potato and Helmet.

Visitors are also attracted to the grand scenery at this southern end of the park and to the many historic mining relics. Other people come for the fishing, which is extremely worthwhile – Schouten Island and the western side of Freycinet are easily accessible by small boats.

SOUTHWEST NATIONAL PARK

Majestic Wilderness Mountains and Coast

Established in 1953, the Southwest National Park is a land of misty peaks and lofty jagged ranges separated by plunging, forested valleys. Sweeping saturated Button Grass sedgelands cover the foothills and lowlands while perched cirque lakes and wilderness rivers drain from the dramatic interior to a wild coastline. Bathurst Harbour and Port Davey are spectacular fiord-like waterways extending deep into the park.

Equal in status to the wildernesses of Patagonia in southern Chile, and the Fiordland National Park of New Zealand, this park in the south-west of Tasmania draws walkers from all over the world. A spectacular long-distance walking track traverses the park's 6,083 square kilometres (2,348 square miles) of wilderness.

The park is bordered to the south and west by the crashing Southern Ocean coast and to the north by the Franklin–Gordon Wild Rivers National Park. Along with Franklin–Gordon Wild Rivers, the Southwest is part of the Tasmanian Wilderness World Heritage Area, which was listed in 1982 and extended in 1989.

Vegetation of the Southwest

Landform, soils, frost, fire and rain have produced a wonderful mosaic of vegetation in the park, with more than 175 endemic species. The sharply pointed peaks of hard white quartzite and rust-coloured dolerite face the rain-laden Roaring Forties, and the area receives 3,000 millimetres (120 inches) and more of rain annually.

Above right: The endangered Orange-bellied Parrot breeds in summer in the moorlands of south-western Tasmania.

The soils are generally thin, sandy, infertile and saturated, and the region is covered by Button Grass sedge, Tea Tree, Dog Rose and, in slightly drier places, impenetrable Horizontal Scrub. This plant grows tall on a weak stem, which falls over to weave an impenetrable mesh with surrounding plants of the same species.

Areas of protected eastern and northern aspects, or deep hollows where better soil has accumulated, support stands of lowland rainforest consisting mainly of Myrtle Beech, mosses, lichens and ferns. Three endemic conifers thrive in the Southwest National Park – King Billy Pine, Celery Top Pine and the exalted Huon Pine, prized by woodworkers for its fine pale yellow, aromatic softwood. Some Huon Pines have lived for well over 1,000 years.

Eucalypts have taken over parts of the beech community, probably after the local Aboriginal people began burning areas of land, to 'clean' the country and for hunting purposes, following the decline of the last ice age some 15,000 years ago. Few local Aboriginal people survived imprisonment by colonial authorities after European contact.

Wilderness Wildlife

If the marsupial Tasmanian Tiger (Thylacine) still survives it will probably be somewhere here in the mysterious, misty world of the rugged south-west. Other creatures abound, however, and sunning in the crowns of the Button Grass could be any of Tasmania's three snakes, most probably the Island Tiger Snake, which lives primarily on frogs and yabbies and the occasional rare Swamp Antechinus, a tiny mouse-sized marsupial.

Map labels: Gordon R.; Strathgordon; Serpentine Dam; To Hobart; Lake Pedder; Mt Anne; Southwest National Park; Scotts Peak Dam; Hobart; Port Davey Track; Federation Peak; Port Davey; Bathurst Harbour; Melaleuca; N; South Coast Walking Track; Catamaran; SOUTHERN OCEAN

Location: The park extends across south-west Tasmania south of Lake Gordon and 110 km (68 miles) south-west of Hobart.

Climate: Wet and windy all year. Driest in February, 125 mm (5 inches); wettest in August, 250 mm (9 inches); warmest December–January, 10–20° C (50–68° F); coldest in June, 4–13° C (40–54° F). Mountains much wetter and colder. Blizzards can occur any month.

When to Go: November–March; at other times floods and snow may cause frequent delays.

Access: Only road into park is to Scotts Peak Dam, Lake Pedder, and Serpentine Dam. Peripheral road-heads at Cockle Creek, Tahune Forest Reserve and road C607 into the Mt Anne area. Light aircraft strip at Melaleuca Ranger Station. Safe yacht/boat anchorage at Port Davey.

Permits: Register routes and obtain camping permits from Melaleuca and Scotts Peak ranger stations or national parks office, Hobart.

Equipment: First-class walking, camping and climbing gear. Large-scale maps, compass and/or GPS instrument, warm clothing, wind jacket, rain gear, first-aid kit, insect repellent, hat, torch and spare batteries, fuel stove and fuel.

Facilities: Walking tracks with designated campsites, two basic huts at Melaleuca for 20 people. Car camping areas with full facilities at Cockle Creek and fewer facilities at Edger Dam, Scotts Peak Dam and Tahune. Rainforest nature track, Junction Hill.

Watching Wildlife: Waterbirds about lagoons; Orange-bellied and Ground parrots and Beautiful Firetail Finches on moorlands; docile venomous snakes coiled on Button Grass. Most mammals nocturnal.

Visitor Activities: Walking, boat fishing on Lake Pedder, scenic flights, boat cruises on Bathurst Harbour and Port Davey, wildlife study, mountain climbing.

Right: *The south-west coast of Tasmania near Port Davey is beaten by the gales of the Roaring Forties.*

Below: *The Eastern Quoll, or Eastern Native Cat, recently extinct on the mainland, is still common in Tasmania, probably because there are no foxes on the island.*

park's White-breasted Sea Eagles, Wedge-tailed Eagles and Peregrine Falcons soar in the westerly winds.

Tracks into the Wilderness

The names of the south-west mountains declare their character – Snowy and Ironbound Ranges, The White Monolith, The Jupiter, The Razorback, Precipitous Bluff, Folded Range and Lost World Plateau. The only walking track through this rugged wilderness begins at Cockle Creek, Catamaran, in the park's south-east. The famous South Coast Walking Track skirts the coastal headlands and beaches to Prion Bay. A diversion climbs to the spectacular top of Precipitous Bluff (1,219 metres/3,398 feet) before returning across limestone slopes through forests of exceedingly tall Mountain Ash (80 metres/262 feet high), to New River Lagoon.

After a long wade back to the main track on the beach, it is another 55 kilometres across high ranges and Button Grass plains to the Melaleuca Ranger Station on Bathurst Harbour. Many walkers fly in or out from here, making the trip a 75-kilometre (47-mile) walk, taking anywhere between five and nine days. Across the Bathurst Narrows the track becomes the Port Davey Track, diving inland to Scotts Peak Dam and the roadhead at Lake Pedder, a further 60 kilometres or four to five days. From the Arthur Plains a very rugged track takes an alternate route to a forestry roadhead at Tahune Forest Reserve.

Opposite: *Brilliant green cushion plants and palm-like* Richeas *are confined to Tasmania's subalpine areas.*

Wombats are also often seen ambling through the bush, while the Bennett's Wallaby and the smaller Pademelon have created grazing 'lawns' near creeks and lakes. At night, Brushtail and Ringtail possums, Tiger Cats (Spotted-tailed Quolls) and the smaller Native Cats (Eastern Quolls) forage and hunt while the Tasmanian Devil prefers to scavenge as well as hunt.

The beautiful Orange-bellied Parrot, one of the world's rarest birds, summers in the sedgelands of the Southwest, as does another very rare parrot, the unusual Ground Parrot. Beautiful Firetail finches, Striated Fieldwrens and the Dusky Robin make the more open habitats of the park their home while, high above, the

MOUNT FIELD NATIONAL PARK

A Pocket of Scenic Diversity

Mount Field National Park, just 80 kilometres (50 miles) north-west of Hobart, protects 170 square kilometres (65.6 square miles) of extremely diverse landscapes. The park spreads across a cluster of mountains north of the Gordon River Road and encompasses some of the tallest wet eucalypt forests anywhere in the world, classic glaciated landscapes, wilderness sub alpine lands, beautiful waterfalls in pristine settings, glorious wildflowers in season and a feast of possible wildlife contact. Mount Field even has a small ski field.

Agitation for a national park to cover the Russell Falls area, established as a scenic reserve in 1885 and now part of the park, led to the passage of the Tasmanian Scenery Preservation Act in 1915. In 1916, Mount Field National Park and Freycinet National Park, on the east coast, were established, becoming Tasmania's first two national parks.

Ice Power

Mount Field West, at 1,434 metres (4,704 feet), is the highest of a cluster of dolerite peaks in the park from which a number of broad U-shaped valleys radiate. At the climax of the ice ages an ice cap fed by westerly blizzards rested over this knot of mountains. Tongues of ice-carrying boulders and gravels of dolerite slowly moved down from the rim into the valleys, grinding, plucking, shoving and transporting rock as glaciers do.

Opposite: *Glacial lakes and tarns, habitat for endemic aquatic fauna, are scattered across Mount Field NP.*

Above right: *Mountain Gentian in Tasmania's subalpine sod tussock grassland flowers from February to March.*

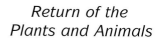

Dumped at the glaciers' snouts the moraines dammed up many valleys and formed lakes Fenton, Dobson, Seal, Belcher and others. Where the icesheet dropped over a long terrace of dolerite, the exquisite series of shallow tarns along the Tarn Shelf were torn out. The circuit walk from Lake Dobson through sub-alpine wet heath and along this picturesque shelf offers fabulous views of Mount Bridges and of Lake Seal with its classic curving glacial morainesis and is one of the best ways to experience the variety of landscape in the park.

Return of the Plants and Animals

As the ice retreated and warmer conditions returned, water from the thaw etched detail into the ice-sculpted landscape, and plants and animals gradually moved back from lower altitudes and warmer refuges. Today, the mosaic of vegetation is a record of environmental conditions over the past millennium.

The minutiae of the high country is unbelievably beautiful, with its fabulous combination of textures and colours – even the smell of the air, accented by the Lemon-scented Boronia. Notable plants include the cushion plants of the high moorlands, which frequently harbour Gentians and sundews, and the Sphagnum crowding the edge of tarns. Most intriguing of all, however, are the varied characters of the bonsai plants such as the Native Strawberry, a dwarf creeping pine (*Microcachrys sp.*) with a juicy red and succulent cone much loved by the Black Currawong, struggling for life on the rocky moors. Small as they are, these plants are frequently found to be of a great age. The highlands also harbour a living fossil unaltered for 200 million years – the Tasmanian Mountain Shrimp, abundant in the tarns.

Location: 75 km (47 miles) west of Hobart, the State capital, within the Derwent River catchment.

Climate: Cool, damp summers with dramatic weather changes (even occasional blizzards) and many fogs; cold winters with blizzards on the high country above Lake Fenton.

When to Go: Winter is the best time to visit for skiing and alpine recreations, October–December is best for wildflowers, and anytime from November–April is fine for walking and driving. Russell Falls can be visited at any time.

Access: By sealed road from Hobart to the park entrance at Russell Falls, then unsealed road to Lake Dobson which is subalpine. In winter, snow chains must be carried for the National Park to Lake Dobson road.

Permits: Camping permit and Lake Dobson Hut and lodge bookings available from park visitor centre. Summer fire restrictions.

Equipment: Warm clothing and wet weather gear, daypack with extra clothing for weather changes, hat, sunscreen, camping gear, fuel stove and fuel, strong walking boots suitable for wet walking, ski gear, large-scale map, compass.

Facilities: Self-guided nature walks at Russell Falls and Lake Dobson, Lyrebird and Pandani Grove; day walks along marked routes. Roadside information bays. Visitor information centre and kiosk, powered caravan/camping area with all facilities, basic cabins at Lake Dobson. Skiing services at Mount Mawson in winter. Five trackside bushwalking survival huts.

Watching Wildlife: Best seen along self-guided nature walks. Brushtail Possums, wallabies and Pademelons can be spotted around campsites and Lake Dobson; Lyrebirds in fern areas and forests; Platypus in lakes and streams at sunrise and dusk.

Visitor Activities: Car touring, walking, skiing and ice skating.

Above: *Common Brushtail Possums,* Trichosurus vulpecula, *have learned to live close to humans and are frequently seen at night.*

Right: *Ice-scraped hollows now form the shallow tarns surrounded by heath and Pencil Pines,* Athrotaxis cupressoides, *on the park's magnificent Tarn Shelf.*

Life Below the Treeline

Most of the animals in the park are found below the tree-line, with habitats varying according to changes in altitude. Each habitat shelters different fauna, from the exquisitely formed native pines – King Billy, Celery-top and Pencil –at the highest level down through the gaunt Snow Gums to the silent glens smothered in Myrtle Beech, aromatic Sassafras and Yellow Gums. Finally, towering wet eucalypt forests of Mountain Ash and Ribbon Gums flourish by the streams and lakes. Brushtail Possums inhabit the forest country, Ringtail Possums the thick gully scrub and Myrtle, while the Southern Pygmy Possum frequents heathy flowering places.

Wombats are widespread, escaping the cold in their burrows and, in the same way, the Broad Toothed Rat makes its warmer runways and nest deep within the moorland vegetation among rocks. Platypus live in the larger streams, lakes and tarns although they are elusive creatures and often difficult to spot. The park also supports several active carnivores – the Tasmanian Devil, a scavenger, and the Tiger Cat (Spotted-tailed Quoll) and Native Cat (Eastern Quoll) – both of which feed on small mammals, birds and carrion.

Right: *Tasmanian Pademelons can be seen in large numbers on grassy clearings near forest along the Russell Falls track.*

Birds in the park include Green Rosellas, Brown Scrub Wrens, the Scrub Tit and Tasmanian Thornbill and more than 50 other species common to the mainland as well. The Superb Lyrebird, introduced from Victoria in 1934, is very active in the wet forests. It can be spotted amongst the massive tree ferns around Russell Falls, near the entrance to the park, and in the tall Swamp Gum Forest nearby. In 1949 a major environmental controversy blew up when 15 square kilometres (5.8 square miles) of these Swamp Gums – including some of the world's tallest flowering trees, many rising to 100 metres (328 feet) – were excised for woodpulp production.

FRANKLIN–GORDON WILD RIVERS NATIONAL PARK

A Defining Wilderness

Around 185 kilometres north-west of Hobart, the Lyell Highway crosses the King William Range between the Derwent and Franklin headwaters into the Franklin–Gordon Wild Rivers National Park. Furious rivers roar through mighty chasms of polished quartzite and cavernous limestone, fracturing a maze of wild forested ranges that are more often in mist than in sun.

Parts of the area were already protected as Frenchmans Cap National Park (established in 1939) and the Lower Gordon Scenic Reserve (established in 1908) when environmentalists Dr Bob Brown and Paul Smith made their two-week raft trip down the Franklin in 1975. This experience inspired them to lead the epic protest against a second dam on the Gordon River. Australia's most dramatic environmental battle resulted in the establishment of the Franklin–Gordon Wild Rivers National Park, 4,408 square kilometres (1,700 square miles) in area, in 1981.

Bordered by the famous Cradle Mountain–Lake St Clair National Park to the north and the rugged Southwest National Park to the south, this remote park is now part of the Tasmanian Wilderness World Heritage Area, which was listed in 1982 and extended in 1989. According to Bob Brown, the area stands as 'a living memorial to all those other wild rivers that have been dammed, diverted, polluted and changed'.

Above right: *Rafting the raging Franklin River is one of Australia's most exhilarating wilderness experiences.*

A Pristine Wilderness

With only a few tracks through sections of this wild park, the best way to explore the magnificence of the area is to take a two-week organized rafting trip down the Franklin, although a high level of fitness is required. For those of only moderate fitness, the lower Franklin–Gordon runs much more slowly through magnificent gorges and forests.

The river begins in high moor bogs amid mounds of cushion plants, Sphagnum, Button Grass, Creeping Pines, Tea Trees, and deciduous Southern Beech before sliding via tarns and lakes into a more defined course. Once the watering place for Tasmanian Tigers (Thylacines), and home for thousands of years to the Tasmanian Aboriginal people, the largest animals to drink here today are Tasmanian Devils, Wombats and Bennett's Wallabies. Platypus are common in quiet pools, foraging about the bed and snags for crayfish and other aquatic invertebrates.

The river gathers strength from numerous tributaries, some draining off the majestic bulk of Frenchmans Cap (1,444 metres/4,736 feet), with its tri-cornered top of gleaming white quartzite. A spectacular walk, three to five days return along a sometimes very boggy track, leads from the Lyell Highway to the top of this great peak.

Carving a mammoth sweep around the mountain, the Franklin plunges between the 'glass-walled cliffs' of the Great Ravine – polished orange and cream translucent quartzite that is never dry. Enormous boulders

Location: 185 km (115 miles) north-west of Hobart, 35 km (21.7 miles) south-east of Strahan on Macquarie Harbour.

Climate: Wet throughout the year (3,000-4,000 mm/118–158 inches per year). Cold winters with snow lying on the ground for 2–5 months in the high country; cool summers. Blizzards at any time in the high country, especially in winter.

When to Go: For walking or rafting, December–March. For boating on the Macquarie Harbour and lower Gordon from Strahan, anytime.

Access: By road to Gordon Dam, or via Lyell Hwy to Frenchmans Cap Track in the north, daily tour boat from Strahan to Gordon River.

Permits: Camping permit from national parks office, Hobart. Walkers and rafters must register with parks service for their own safety.

Equipment: Specialized backpacking gear and/or rafting gear, warm clothing, rain gear, hat, food plus emergency extra food, GPS equipment, compass and large-scale maps, walking boots suitable for walking in water and mud, first-aid kit, insect repellent, fuel stove and fuel.

Facilities: Wilderness campsites and flying-fox crossing of Franklin River on Frenchmans Cap track, emergency hut at Lake Tahune. Franklin River Nature Trail. Commercial accommodation, full facility camping/caravan park, boat hire and boat tours at Strahan.

Watching Wildlife: Macquarie Harbour, lower Gordon and Franklin Rivers rich in river life, birds and bank animals. Frenchmans Cap walkers will see snakes closeup on Button Grass, mammals around campsites and Platypus in Lake Vera.

Visitor Activities: Car touring the periphery, canoeing the lower Gordon–Franklin, boat cruising the lower Gordon, rafting the Franklin, nature study, walking.

dislodged from far above block the raging river, keeping the narrow air space always misty. Growing from litter-filled crevices and soil pockets, 2,000-year-old Huon Pines and ancient beech trees hang out over the canyon and Yellow-tailed Black Cockatoos with lazy wing beats raucously argue over the cones on a pine.

Damming the Gordon

As the Franklin drops towards the sea, its honey-coloured waters become less violent, eventually joining the lower Gordon River on its way to Macquarie Harbour. From Strahan, on Macquarie Harbour, visitors seeking a more civilized experience take floatplane joyflights over the park, or wilderness boat cruises up the lower Gordon to Heritage Landing. The upper Gordon was dammed in 1972, as part of Tasmania's biggest hydro-electric scheme, before the nationwide resistance that saved the Franklin was organized. From high snowy ranges, across broad Button Grass moors, this river once drifted freely through beautiful Lake Pedder, now drowned, before crashing through the incredible canyon of The Gordon Splits and past Angel Cliffs on its journey to the sea.

Shadows of the Past

The river ripples across a smooth mosaic of broad pebble beds swept down from the ancient glacial moraines. For 20,000 years or more, black feet walked these icy

Top: *Daisies dot the subalpine slopes of Frenchmans Cap.*

Top left: *The Gordon River loops its way through the dense forest wilderness below the Spence River confluence.*

Left: *Transcendence Reach is one of the few placid sections along the Franklin River's mighty Great Ravine.*

Opposite top: *The Franklin River's tributaries also cut through cool temperate rainforests of Myrtle and treeferns.*

beds – Aboriginal women and children bearing net bags full of mussels, crayfish, small mammals, fruits, seeds, flowers and succulent roots and tubers.

The people living a life locked in by ice – gathering in Kutikina Cave and some of the other 60 Franklin caves, warmed by campfires, sheltering from the bitter cold and sleeting rain. Today, these caves hold the oldest known remnants of ice-age occupation found anywhere in the world. In less than a cubic metre (35.3 cubic feet) of floor, more than 40,000 stone artefacts and 35 kilograms (77 pounds) of bone fragments have been excavated.

Tasmanian Aboriginal people, survivors of early mistreatment by European settlers, are reclaiming their hidden ancestry and today welcome the park and world heritage status of their own sacred mountain places.

Above: Richea scoparia *belongs to the heather family and is one of six* Richea *found in the high wet areas of Tasmania.*

CRADLE MOUNTAIN –LAKE ST CLAIR NATIONAL PARK

A Glaciated Landscape

Like great haystacks they rise above a plateau of glaciated benches, tarns, lakes and deep valleys – Cradle Mountain, Barn Bluff, Eldon Bluff, Pelion West, Ossa and Olympus. This is the highest group of mountains in Tasmania, gouged by ice from the area's hard, fluted dolerite around 20,000 years ago.

Winding across the plateau, the magnificent Overland Track – the most famous walk in Australia – traverses the park from Cradle Mountain in the far north to Lake St Clair, 80 kilometres (50 miles) away to the south.

Today, 1,609 square kilometres (621 square miles) of this dramatic country is protected within the Cradle Mountain–Lake St Clair National Park. Located 90 kilometres (56 miles) inland from Devonport on the north coast, the closest village to this highland park is tiny Derwent Bridge on the southern boundary, eight kilometres (five miles) south of Lake St Clair. First dedicated a national park in 1922, Cradle Mountain–Lake St Clair joined the Franklin–Gordon Wild Rivers and the Southwest national parks in becoming part of the 13,800 square kilometres (5,326 square miles) of the Tasmanian Wilderness World Heritage Area when the Area was created in 1982.

Opposite: Cradle Mountain, its dolerite columnar crown reflected in Dove Lake, is the park's famous northern feature.

Above right: The Tasmanian Devil is the largest surviving carnivorous marsupial – it is common in the park.

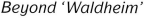

Map labels: Cradle Mtn Lodge; Waldheim; Cradle Mtn; R. Forth; Overland Track; Mt Ossa; Murchison R.; Eldon R.; Cradle Mountain-Lake St Clair National Park; Lake St Clair; N; Cynthia Bay; Derwent Bridge; Hobart

The Overland Track

The track began life as a route through the wilderness for trappers hunting Tasmanian Tigers (Thylacines), now thought to be extinct. Today, the (summertime) five-day walk from Cradle Mountain to Lake St Clair offers lasting memories of a spectacular natural heritage area.

The walk is so popular that over 100,000 pairs of enthusiastic feet have caused considerable damage to the bogs and Button Grass plains. The Tasmanian parks service has responded by setting boardwalks along much of the route and doubling the number of huts. Four of those huts are commercially run, supplying comfortable overnight accommodation and food for guided walks. Day walks around Waldheim and Cynthia Bay at either end of the track allow visitors with limited time or fitness to experience the area in bite-size chunks.

Beyond 'Waldheim'

Once the home and guesthouse of Austrian migrant Gustav Weindorfer, who campaigned vigorously and successfully for a national park in his beloved mountains, 'Waldheim' is the northern terminus for the Overland Track.

Soon after leaving Waldheim the track forks, the western fork climbing past Crater Lake to Marions Lookout 400 metres (1,312 feet) above the beautiful glacial Dove Lake. Off to the right, tucked below the rocketing brown dolerite columns of Cradle Mountain, the chill water of a small hanging lake drops in a wispy

Location: On the Central Highlands 176 km (109 miles) north-west of Hobart and 90 km (56 miles) south of Devonport, on the north coast.

Climate: Cool temperate; wet every month (average annual rainfall 2,000 mm, 80 inches), wettest from April–October. Blizzards any time but common from April–October. Weather changes dramatically with major temperature change.

When to Go: December–March; for rest of year weather very uncertain.

Access: By road from Hobart via Lyell Highway to Derwent Bridge and Cynthia Bay or from northern centres to Waldheim.

Permits: Camping and walking track fees and hut/lodge bookings available from the visitor information centre at the northern park entrance or ranger station at Cynthia Bay, or the national parks office in Hobart.

Equipment: Adequate food with some reserve, warm clothing, wind jacket, rain gear, hat, strong walking boots suitable for wet walking, first-aid kit, sunscreen, insect repellent, binoculars, large-scale map.

Facilities: Walking tracks and boardwalks, interpreted nature tracks, limited survival hut accommodation and commercial huts for guided walks (it is advisable to book early), ranger service. Visitor information centre at Cradle Valley, Ranger Station at Cynthia Bay, camping areas at both.

Watching Wildlife: Opportunistic sightings of 80-plus bird species. Most of the 20 mammal species are nocturnal; Bennett's Wallaby, Tasmanian Pademelons, Brushtail Possums, Wombats and the black Island Tiger Snake will be seen. Echidnas and Platypus are common.

Visitor Activities: Walking, rock climbing, camping, fishing.

Above: *Walkers negotiate a suspension bridge along the famous Overland Track.*

Below: *Tasmania's Bennett's Wallaby is similar to the mainland's Red-necked Wallaby but has thicker fur.*

stream into the forested end of Dove Lake. From the lookout the track passes through subalpine heath, masses of brilliant green cushion plants, beautifully weather-pruned Tea Trees, daisies, red-fruited Mountain Rocket, Richea heath, mallee and a hundred other struggling species. Soon the slopes of Cradle Mountain begin to recede as the colossal stone stack of Barn Bluff rises shear from the heath-covered, smoothly glaciated 'pavement' five kilometres (3.1 miles) away.

Artists Pool

The second route around monumental Cradle Mountain skirts Dove Lake to the east across ice-scraped pavements and cascading beech-lined creeks, through woodland and forest with views down Hansons River into the depths of the Forth Gorge. Artists Pool is a fine example of the thousands of tarns which dot the landscape. Its clear, tea-coloured waters reflect the mountain in a picture framed by ancient gnarled Pencil Pines, veterans of many blizzards. The combination of greens, from subtle to brilliant, and blue-grey boulders encrusted with pale grey lichens beside shining water, all cupped in the curving face of Cradle Mountain, is breathtaking. The textures, too, make this a magical place — mossy carpets, spiky bushes and hummocky shrubs contrast with fuzzy green masses of pine needles and deeply furrowed pine bark.

Wildlife and Plant Highlights

Highlights along the Overland Track remain unblemished despite the increase in foot traffic. The view from the

northern ridge above Lake Windermere across a spectacular writhing mass of gaunt, bleached fire-killed scrub and a mosaic of Button Grass, tarns and woodland to the pale blue waters is sheer joy. Beyond lie the walls of Mount Pelion West and, to the east, Mount Oakleigh's salmon-coloured fluted columnar cliffs. An evening in Windermere Hut – crammed to the brim with fellow walkers, buffeted by the wind and flapping trees and at the mercy of pack-foraging Brushtail Possums and Wombats bumping cans – is equally unforgettable.

After skirting the slopes of Mount Pelion West, covered with flowering Tea Trees and rushing creeks, the track emerges onto sunlit tarn-flecked moors before plunging into the silent depths of a Myrtle Beech forest with a floor of mosses, lichens and ferns. Tasmanian Tigers (Thylacines) once hunted in these habitats but, today, the largest carnivores are the hyena-like Tasmanian Devil and the Tiger Cat (Spotted-tailed Quoll).

Further on, among the eucalypt scrub, scarlet blooms of Tasmanian Waratahs provide tiny explosions of colour

beneath the massive dolerite crown of Mount Ossa – at 1,617 metres (5,304 feet), Tasmania's highest peak.

Lake St Clair

Du Cane Hut, a classic track hut also known as 'Windsor Castle', was built by a hunter-prospector in 1910 of shingles and boards split from the straight-grained King Billy Pines nearby. From this point the track crosses the divide into the long glacial valley of the Narcissus River and Lake St Clair. A ferry runs the 20 kilometres (12.4 miles) from Narcissus Hut downlake to Cynthia Bay – the ranger station at the end of the Overland Track – cutting the duration of the walk by a day. However, when the weather is fine the lakeshore walk provides a visual feast, passing through rainforest and giant *Richea* stands with sudden 'windows' opening onto a sublime lakescape with Mount Ida as a backdrop.

Overleaf: *A rare winter view of tranquil Artists Pool with Cradle Mountain and Little Horn in the background.*

Above: *Boardwalks along most of the Overland Track protect bogs from erosion.*

Below: *Kia Ora Hut is one of the commercial huts along the Overland Track.*

SOUTH AUSTRALIA

South Australia, 984,000 square kilometres (379,824 square miles) in area, stretches north from the wild Southern Ocean to the desert country in the centre of the continent. Around 80 per cent of the land in this, the driest State in Australia, receives less than 250 millimetres (10 inches) of rain per year. After rain the outback is ablaze with a carpet of wildflowers.

The coastline extends for 3,700 kilometres (2,298 miles) along the Great Australian Bight, dipping into two great gulfs near Adelaide, the State capital. Kangaroo Island, Australia's largest, lies across Gulf St Vincent. The western end of the island forms the Flinders Chase National Park, filled with wildlife that is safe from mainland predators and home to a colony of New Zealand Fur Seals.

South Australia has two mountainous regions – the granite Musgraves, along the Northern Territory border, and the Flinders Ranges complex, running northwards from the Fleurieu Peninsula to fade into the desert near salt Lake Eyre. A vast arc of salt lakes begins just north of the Spencer Gulf and swings around the northern Flinders Ranges. These ranges form a major biogeographic boundary for both wildlife and vegetation. They are protected in part by two important parks – the Flinders Ranges National Park, containing the famous Wilpena Pound, a spectacular rock basin edged with golden quartzite crags, and the Gammon Ranges National Park, the rugged homeland of the beautiful Yellow-footed Rock Wallaby. Red Kangaroos flourish in the semi-arid grassy plains and shrublands around the ranges.

Australia's largest river system, the Murray–Darling, drains from all three eastern States until finally the Murray alone flows through South Australia, reaching the sea through a series of large lagoons south of Adelaide. In the north-east, the Georgina and Diamantina rivers and Cooper Creek periodically flood from tropical rains in Queensland and spread into an amazing network of channels, lakes and billabongs en route to the Lake Eyre depression (−15.2 metres, −50 feet), which they occasionally reach. Nearby, Witjira National Park provides a fascinating experience of arid-land Australia, with the added attraction of the Dalhousie Springs.

FLINDERS CHASE NATIONAL PARK

Kangaroo Island's Wild West End

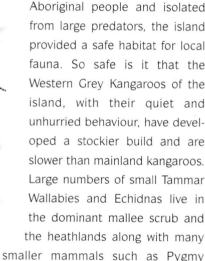

Established in 1919, Flinders Chase National Park covers much of the western end of Kangaroo Island. The island is Australia's third largest, separated from the Fleurieu Peninsula south of Adelaide by the narrow Backstairs Passage. The park is 737 square kilometres (284 square miles) in area and spreads across a gently undulating plateau of perched dunes on a base of hard granite and metamorphic rock, bounded to the west by the wild seas of the Southern Ocean.

From the heights of the plateau the Rocky River has cut a deep gorge on its way to Maupertuis Bay. Sometimes a wild cascading stream, sometimes a string of long limpid pools of tea-coloured water overhung by Swamp and Manna gums and by Tea Tree dripping with tiny white flowers, the Rocky River is the largest of the park's waterways.

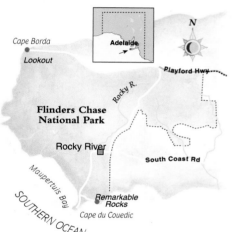

Vegetation in the park varies from mixed forest growing along the creeks and wetter areas to dry mallee scrub on the uplands. Coastal heathlands spread inland from Cape du Couedic in the south and above the park's rugged coastline. Open

Opposite: Salt-laden sea winds sculpted these Remarkable Rocks – granite tors covered with brilliantly coloured lichens.

Above right: Populations of the island's once-endangered Australian Sea Lions, Neophoca cinerea, are increasing.

Previous pages

P112: *The Heysen Range – named after watercolourist, Sir Hans Heysen – typifies the drama and colour of the Flinders.*
P113: *The striking Sturt's Desert Pea, Clianthus formosus.*

grasslands are grazed by large numbers of kangaroos and Cape Barren Geese. Wildlife abounds in the park as the island is free of mainland predators and is readily seen around the Rocky River visitor centre.

A Natural Sanctuary

Kangaroo Island was cut off from the mainland by rising sea levels nearly 10,000 years ago. Deserted by the Aboriginal people and isolated from large predators, the island provided a safe habitat for local fauna. So safe is it that the Western Grey Kangaroos of the island, with their quiet and unhurried behaviour, have developed a stockier build and are slower than mainland kangaroos. Large numbers of small Tammar Wallabies and Echidnas live in the dominant mallee scrub and the heathlands along with many smaller mammals such as Pygmy Possums and Southern Brown Bandicoots.

Reports of abundant wildlife and seal colonies led American sealers to settle on the island in 1803. It is fortunate that they, along with subsequent settlers, did not introduce the rabbit or the fox and that they left the wild western end and the weather-beaten south undisturbed. As wildlife came under siege elsewhere in South Australia – the Toolache Wallaby was probably extinct by 1924 – Flinders Chase became a sanctuary for hard-pressed mainland species. Mallee Fowl, Koalas, Platypus and Cape Barren Geese were released and have flourished on the island and in the park. Today, picnickers at Rocky River are fenced in from the always inquisitive kangaroos and Emus, while at night campers are visited by Brushtail Possums looking for a handout.

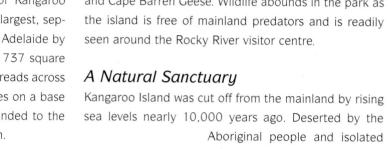

Location: Western end of Kangaroo Island, 90 km (56 miles) west of Kingscote and 200 km (124 miles) south-west of Adelaide.

Climate: Cool Mediterranean with cool, wet windy winters and warm dry summers.

When to Go: Anytime but best August–April. Best for wildflowers, August–November; best for swimming and fishing, October–April.

Access: To island by air from Adelaide to Kingscote; coach and cars by ferry from Cape Jervis. On island, road access to park from Penneshaw, American River and Kingscote via the Playford Highway or the South Coast Road. Hire cars available from the island's towns.

Permits: Camping permits and bookings for lighthouse cottages available from national park service, Adelaide or Kingscote.

Equipment: Camping equipment, strong walking shoes or boots, hat, sunscreen, fishing gear, swimming gear, binoculars, warm clothing, windjacket, rain gear.

Facilities: Car campground (no power), picnic facilities, visitor information centre, ranger service, walking tracks and lookouts, limited water, school group accommodation, historic farmhouse and lighthouse cottages in park to rent. Full accommodation in towns on the eastern end of island.

Watching Wildlife: Abundant wildlife in Flinders Chase including kangaroos, Koalas, Spiny Anteaters, Wombats, Platypus, seals, Cape Barren Geese, parrots and honeyeaters. Wildflowers best from August–November. A number of other Conservation Parks on the island are located nearby.

Visitor Activities: Camping, wildlife discovery and viewing, photography of seascapes and wildlife, sketching, day walks, overnight walks, beach and rock fishing, swimming.

Rings of bright water spread across the shining pools along Rocky River as Platypus surface during their early morning and dusk forays for crustaceans and dragonfly nymphs among the bottom snags and pebbles. A gentle stroll along the Black Stump walking track from the Rocky River picnic area leads to a special Platypus viewing area. Koalas sway high up in the Ribbon Gums along Rocky River during the day while at night a variety of

grunts, snuffles or excited squeals identify sparring male Koalas bickering over their next mate. In fact, Koalas have been so successful on the island that many eucalypt food trees have been severely damaged and animals are now being removed to stock mainland areas.

Birdlife Abounds

In spring, the broad coastal heathlands and the mallee burst into flower and with the flow of nectar comes the honey-eating birds. The multi-coloured lorikeets – the Little, Musk, Purple-crowned and Rainbow – and the Brown-headed, Singing, White-eared, White-plumed, New Holland and Eastern Spinebill honeyeaters all flock to the rich reds and pinks of the bottlebrushes, the tawny banksias, the creamy spikes of the Grasstrees, spectacular flowering eucalypts, paperbarks, Native Fuchsias, epacrids, Rice Flowers and many others.

Waterbirds such as Black Swans, Australian Pelicans and waders proliferate on the island's lagoons while Bronzewing Pigeons, robins and Variegated Wrens flit about the shrublands and mallee scrub. The national park is also home to an isolated population of rare Glossy Black Cockatoos and Western Whipbirds. The large silhouettes of these cockatoos are frequently seen as they move about the park on lazy wings to the accompaniment of their melancholy raucous cry.

Above: *Cape Barren Geese,* Ceriopsis novaehollandiae, *have no close living relatives. They nest among grass tussocks on southern offshore islands such as Kangaroo Island.*

Above right: *The Tammar Wallaby,* Macropus eugenii, *is abundant on the island, sheltering in dense scrub, and feeding out on grassland after dark.*

Left: *The Southern Ocean has carved Admirals Arch from the rocky shoreline at Cape du Couedic in the park's south-west.*

Cape du Couedic and the Coast

Now that the lighthouses are automated, the Park Service leases out the lighthouse keepers' cottages at Cape du Couedic to visitors. This is the perfect base for those who wish to study the hour-by-hour antics of the resident New Zealand Fur Seals. The muffled roar of the sea can no longer hide the excited high-pitched barking of the steadily growing colony, finally making a comeback after the rampant killing sprees of the 19th century. Nearby, the beaches of the island's south, such as Seal Bay, and the rocky shorelines around the cape provide safe habitat for thousands of Australian Fur Seals as well as magnificent Australian Sea Lions.

Here, too, magnificent rockscapes have been carved from the coast by wild winter seas. Mighty Admirals Arch at Cape du Couedic has been sculpted by centuries of wind and wave action, and the Remarkable Rocks, a short drive away, lie as though placed by some giant hand on the domed headland of Kirkpatrick Point. These huge granite tors, painted red with lichen, have been hollowed and sculpted by tireless salt-laden winds and crashing waves. Along the coast, Ospreys and White-bellied Sea Eagles watch over curving white beaches and intricately sea-etched calcarenite clifflines. The West Bay Road takes Rocky River visitors to track heads leading to delightful bays, beaches and coves while the Shackle Track connects with Playford Highway and the Cape Borda Lighthouse.

Top: *The friable limestone (calcarenite) of southern Kangaroo Island dissolves into caverns like this one at West Bay.*

Right: *Sunset warms the now-automated Cape du Couedic lighthouse – the associated cottages are rented to visitors.*

Overleaf: *Harveys Return is one of the many pristine bays awaiting the snorkeller in Flinders Chase National Park.*

FLINDERS RANGES NATIONAL PARK

Inspiration for Artist and Naturalist

The Flinders Ranges run roughly north from the Spencer Gulf through woodland, scrub and grass-land to the edge of the Strzelecki Desert. The forests of deep green Cypress Pines and Hill Coolibahs in the range's cooler and wetter gullies and southern slopes contrast sharply with the grey-green of the mallee, Bluebush and Mulga in the surrounding arid scrub country.

Of the three major national parks in the mountain chain, the Flinders Ranges National Park – located 160 kilometres (100 miles) inland from Port Augusta – is most famous. An expanse of undulating hills spreads across the north-eastern part of the park while, further south, great red lines of broken cliffs and terraces with multicoloured defiles and canyons rise from arid bush-covered plains.

At the southern end of the park, the vast elliptical dished valley of Wilpena Pound is the most recognized place in any South Australian national park. This bowl, edged with golden quartzite crags 500-metres (1,640 feet) high is a place of particular significance to the Adnyamathanha ('people of the hills') Aboriginal people. The Pound was part of 'Wilpena' sheep station until 1945 when it became a National Pleasure Resort. In 1972 nearby 'Oraparinna' station was added to Wilpena to create the 900 square kilometres (347 square miles) of today's Flinders Ranges National Park.

Opposite: *The glowing walls of Wilpena Pound enclose a bowl-shaped valley from which only one creek escapes.*

Above right: *Wedge-tailed Eagles, often seen soaring above park cliffs, have wingspans of up to 2.5 metres (8 feet).*

Map labels:
Flinders Ranges National Park
Brachina Gorge
Oraparinna
Bunyeroo Valley
Wilpena Chalet
Pantapinna Ck
To Hawker
N
Adelaide

Land of the Dreamtime Serpents

The Adnyamathanha Aboriginal people believe that in the dreamtime of the distant past two great ancestral serpents, the Akurras (or Arkaru), came from the north and travelled towards the site of a ceremonial gathering among the hills near Wilpena. They camped by a water-hole near a ridge and after dark lifted their heads high up to see over the country. Driving into Wilpena Pound the two dramatic peaks visible up the valley to the north – St Marys Peak and Beatrice Hill – are the heads of the two Akurras.

From their ceremonial campfires people saw the Akurras' eyes glowing above the hills like bright stars. The appearance of these bright stars was the signal for the beginning of the cere-monies. The two Akurras separated to surround the people. Their great bodies quickly encircled the gathering as the Akurras came upon them like powerful whirlwinds and all were devoured except two initiates who escaped to the east. The enclosing walls of the Pound today suggest the coiled bodies of these dreamtime ser-pents. To Europeans this story may seem to link Wilpena with disaster but to the Aboriginal people it is an expla-nation of landforms and spirit places that require respect.

Nature's Boarding Houses

Just as the Pound serves as the lasting image of the Flinders Ranges landscape, so the area's ancient River Red Gum trees stand as its plant icon. These magnificent veterans of flood and storm, hundreds of years old, hang grimly to the edges of Aroona, Brachina and Wilpena creeks as well as most of the other watercourses wind-ing through the park. One particular gum tree will live

Location: In the central Flinders Ranges, 480 km (298 miles) north of Adelaide, and 159 km (99 miles) north-east of Port Augusta.

Climate: Semi-arid; the average annual rainfall of 250–350 mm (9–14") is evenly distributed between summer storms and winter periods of lighter rain. Long, hot summers, cool winters with some frosts. Many cloudless days.

When to Go: Anytime but best in the cooler months from April–October. Flowers from July–September.

Access: Sealed roads to Hawker and Wilpena from Port Augusta, on Highway 1, and Wilmington. All other roads are gravel or clay with the gorge sections best negotiated by 4WD vehicle.

Permits: Camping fee with permits from parks service at Oraparinna park headquarters or Adelaide. Fire bans may be in place.

Equipment: Camping gear, water-bottle (water is available), strong walking shoes or boots, maps, first-aid kit, broad-brimmed hat and sun-screen, film, binoculars.

Facilities: Ranger services, walking tracks and marked routes, camp-sites with minimum facilities, unpowered car campsites, informa-tion centre at Oraparinna and Hawker, Wilpena Motel (bookings from South Australian Tourist Bureau) has kiosk, full accommoda-tion available at Hawker.

Watching Wildlife: Wildlife is ubiqui-tous but Yanyanna and Bunyeroo Gorge tracks are particularly good for spotting. Look out for Red Kangaroos, Euros, Yellow-footed Rock Wallabies and six smaller species of macropod, also 35 species of reptiles, and over 100 bird species including many parrots.

Visitor Activities: Car touring, walk-ing, wildlife watching, birdwatching and botanical studies.

Above: *Flocks of Galahs,* Cacatua roseicapilla, *are often seen beside the road at anytime of day and near water in the evening.*

Right: *The native White Cypress Pine,* Callitris glauca, *is common in the Flinders Ranges.*

Far right: *Australia's largest bird, the flightless Emu,* Dromaius novaehollandiae, *is found throughout Australia's semi-arid lands.*

forever in Harold Cazneaux's famous prize-winning black and white photograph of 1931, 'Spirit of Endurance'.

Down Brachina, Bunyeroo and Edeowie gorges, thousands of Galahs, Little Corellas, Sulphur Crested Cockatoos and Mallee Ringneck Parrots find shelter and nests in the River Red Gum hollows and feed on the buds, flowers, nectar and seed. A waterhole ringed with these sturdy trees, quiet under the brilliant stars of semi-arid Australia, makes the finest of campsites.

The peace of a night under the stars is shattered at dawn (and dusk) with a cacophony of sound from the noisy inhabitants of nature's boarding houses.

Eagles in the Wind

With the warming of the cliffs after sunrise, the cool air along the creeks begins to drift and rise. From a massive stick-nest high in a River Red Gum an old black Wedge-tailed Eagle lifts off. Its younger brown mate soon fol-

lows, rising in long, lazy circles on the heated air. These cousins of the Golden Eagle will soar a thousand and more metres up, searching the ledges with their acute vision for tasty feral goat kids, Yellow-footed Rock Wallabies, young Euros or unwary lizards basking in the sun. Watching these stately birds playing on the wind is a special part of the grand experience of walking and climbing about the high ridges of Wilpena Pound or the ABC Range, so-named because of its 26 peaks. Ornithologists also revel in the park's incredible mix of species – birds from the arid interior mingle with those from the temperate south and others with ranges to the east or the west, over 200 species altogether.

Discovering Akurra's Secrets

The grandeur of the Flinders Ranges makes camping in the park sensational, although there is a motel at Wilpena – a small settlement at the end of the bitumen road on the way into the park. Purple shadows smudge across golden escarpments under an azure sky. The spiky coniferous texture of native Cypress Pines contrasts with the billowing canopies of the River Red Gums and the regiments of lesser eucalypt species marching boldly across the hills. In other places stands of Black Oak show clearly where soils on dolomite have formed. Blonde sun-dried grasses, Grasstrees and acacias (the wattles), lend a true Australian atmosphere.

One of Australia's most famous watercolourists and atmospheric draftsmen, Sir Hans Heysen, gained much of his inspiration from these mountains and their gum trees. So linked is he with the area that a walking track, the Heysen Trail, commencing south of Adelaide, runs the full length of the Flinders Ranges. Graded and marked tracks through the park include robust six-to-10-hour walks to such places as St Marys Peak (Akurra's head), Edeowie Gorge and Black Gap as well as numerous shorter walks to wildlife areas and lookouts. However, high temperatures in summer restrict pleasant walking to between the months of May and October.

Above: *Wilpena Pound stretches into the distance from the walking track to St Mary's Peak.*

Below left: *Aboriginal art covers Arkaroo Rock on the outside of the Pound wall in the Heysen Range.*

GAMMON RANGES NATIONAL PARK

Yellow-footed Rock Wallaby Homeland

Gammon Ranges National Park was created in 1970 from 1,282 square kilometres (495 square miles) of pastoral lease, most of which is magnificent semi-arid mountainscape but very poor sheep country. From the air these lofty ranges – the most northern of the Flinders Ranges, 750 kilometres (466 miles) north of Adelaide – are a spectacular whirlpool of red, yellow, brown and white stone, stirred in concentric circles by a giant hand. Here and there a mosaic of dark green native Cypress Pine, slate-green mallee scrub, russet shrubland, Bluebush and smoky-green Mulga tinges the rugged landscape.

Stretching east from the ranges in a broad corridor to the edge of the vast salt Lake Frome, the Gammon Ranges National Park encompasses a greater diversity of landscape and habitat than any other South Australian park. Salt lake, plains, dunes, gorges, pounds, mountain ranges, plateaux, tree-lined river systems and permanent springs support an equally diverse range of wildlife, including the endangered Yellow-footed Rock Wallaby. The Gammon Ranges and the adjacent Arkaroola lands protect the largest remaining populations of this beautiful creature.

Life in the Wilderness

The Gammon Ranges is one of South Australia's less developed national parks, providing instead an experi-

Opposite: The rugged character of the Gammon Ranges conceals wilderness gorges and ageless Aboriginal art.

Above right: The Yellow-footed Rock Wallaby, Petrogale xanthopus, is perhaps Australia's most beautiful native animal.

ence of extensive wilderness. In this harsh yet beautiful land, gullies, gorges and streams lined with ancient River Red Gums spew forth from the ranges onto the eastern plains of the park to form huge deltaic fans before dying in the blistering white salt of Lake Frome.

For most of the year these streams and gullies are dry. Only rarely, deep in the shadows of the Weetootla, Italowie and Arcoona gorges, the glint of water is seen. Life in the ranges depends upon these permanent waterholes – marked by the presence of the Purple Spotted Gudgeon, a fish of exquisite colouring – and scattered springs. Mountain springs lasting through the worst droughts are the focus of tracks and trails made by Red Kangaroos from the plains, Euros from the hills and Yellow-footed Rock Wallabies from the cliffed terraces and caverns. These wallabies can usually be seen up Balcanoona Creek and other gorge areas in early mornings in spring or, in hotter weather, by water in the evenings at dusk. With its long ring-marked tail, pearly grey body, soft white chest and orange furred feet, the Yellow-footed Rock Wallaby is the most beautiful of the macropods.

Birds, too, gather around the waterholes in the gorges and at the old sheep station dams – snowstorms of Corellas in their tens of thousands, hundreds of Galahs, flocks of Budgerigars and grand lazy winged Red-tailed Black Cockatoos with calls like rusty machines, as well as a host of smaller birds.

Where History Speaks

The Gammon Ranges National Park, though mostly wilderness, is scattered with evidence of people who walked these mountains long ago – mysterious stone cairns, lonely graves by the roadside, rock engravings at

Map labels:
The Needles
Arkaroola
Mainwater Ck
Gammon Ranges National Park
Balcanoona
To Copley
Hawker Hill
To Yunta
Adelaide

Location: In the northern Flinders Ranges, 750 km (466 miles) north of Adelaide, the State capital.

Climate: Arid with cool, dry winters and very hot summers with many days over 35° C (95° F). Chance rain can be intense with flash flooding.

When to Go: April–October for sublime walking days. Wildflowers after heavy rain. Wildlife concentrates near water during droughts.

Access: Good roads to park headquarters at Balcanoona, and to peripheral picnic areas, from Adelaide via Hawker, Copley and Nepabunna or via Yunta and 'Wertaloona'. 4WD tracks within the park. Light aircraft landing strip.

Permits: Camping permits from park headquarters and from parks office at Hawker. Contact ranger before using 4WD roads.

Equipment: Drinking water, first-aid kit, broad-brimmed hat, sunscreen, light clothing with a warm change for winter nights, strong shoes or walking boots, 1:50,000 map sheets as well as a compass or GPS, camping gear, binoculars.

Facilities: Aboriginal ranger service offering intimate knowledge of the park, peripheral picnic areas, 4WD tracks. Hut and 'shearers quarters' accommodation at Balcanoona and outstations, bookings essential at Hawker. Motel and camping area accommodation at Arkaroola. Managed historic mining sites.

Watching Wildlife: Yellow-footed Rock Wallabies can be seen up Balcanoona Creek and other gorge areas in early mornings in spring, or by waters at evening in hotter weather. Euros, Red Kangaroos, Bronzewing Pigeons, Lovely Fairy Wrens and White-Winged Fairy Wrens and Wedge-tailed Eagles are common. Always observe waterholes in silence.

Visitor Activities: Wildlife watching, outback camping, botanical studies, picnicking, 4WD touring, walking.

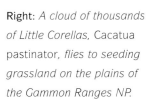

Right: *A cloud of thousands of Little Corellas,* Cacatua pastinator, *flies to seeding grassland on the plains of the Gammon Ranges NP.*

Below: *Fromes Creek gorge is typical Yellow-footed Rock Wallaby habitat.*

Munyi on the hardest quartzite with meanings lost thousands of years ago, a broken pick head.

Four-wheel-drive tracks into remote areas of the park reveal remnants of determined scratchings into the earth – boarded up wells that turned salt; numerous scrapes and shafts where prospectors searched for copper, lead and gold; limestone caverns mined out for bat guano used as fertilizer; towering chimneys crowning ruined copper smelters at Yadnina and Bolla Bollana. And on the heights of Mount McKinlay the recent ruin of an observatory used during the 'International Biophysical Year'.

Experiencing the Gammon Ranges

From park headquarters at Balcanoona, on the edge of the eastern plain, a good gravel road leads west across the ranges through Italowie Gorge. This road climbs beside the gorge into a high, broad valley, crossing and recrossing the creek until it reaches the rolling grassy hills of Nepabunna. This thriving Aboriginal community is home to some of the State's top families of stockman. Today, the park is jointly managed by the Adnyamathanha people. Aboriginal rangers guide visitors and protect the plant and animal resources of the park.

Another good road leads north to Arkaroola – a private resort offering accommodation, a campground, a store and tours. Rough 4WD tracks weave several trails into the high wilderness at the heart of the Gammon Ranges where Arkaroola Creek, Arcoona Creek and Balcanoona Creek rise. This difficult terrain tests even the most prepared of walkers. Here at night when all is silent with only the stars as company the visitor sometimes hears a muffled roar. The local Aboriginal people say that it is Arkaru, the serpent, on his rampaging way, or Mandya, the Euro, blowing to create his habitat.

WITJIRA NATIONAL PARK

Spirit of the Outback

In establishing limits beyond which farming was not allowed, South Australia became the first Australian State to positively act against the accelerated deterioration of its arid areas. Today, over 100,000 square kilometres (38,600 square miles) of these fragile lands are protected in South Australia's national park, conservation park and regional reserve system.

Witjira National Park, with its vast desert landscapes of gibber plains, sand dunes, desiccated tablelands and saltpans, is the most accessible and the most visited of these arid-land places. This is pitiless scorching country in summer but in winter the days are warm and crystal clear with cold clear nights illuminated by brilliant constellations. A journey through this desert wilderness of deep colours and massed flowers after rain, of unexpected wildlife encounters, of silence and harsh beauty produces a strange inner joy.

Impressive though harsh arid environments can be, it is the oasis of Dalhousie Springs that most often draws visitors to this remote yet beautiful area. This unique watery haven overflowing with flora and fauna was first discovered by non-Aboriginal people in 1870, during the construction of the overland telegraph line. Dedicated in 1985, the park's 7,769 square kilometres (3,000 square miles) covers the former Mount Dare Pastoral Lease. The park extends south from the Northern Territory border and is 280 kilometres (174 miles) east of the Stuart Highway that runs from Adelaide to Alice Springs.

Desert Oasis

Deep below the hot dry surface of Witjira National Park lies an enormous reservoir of underground water – the

Above right: *The hardy Native Tomato, Solanum sp., clings to life in the drifting desert sands of Witjira National Park.*

Great Artesian Basin, which spreads beneath 23 per cent of Australia. With over 30,000 bores drilled across the Basin, water pressure has dropped and many springs have ceased to flow. Once an expanse of waving green reeds and large pools of water dotted throughout with the cones of mound springs, the somewhat reduced Dalhousie Springs of Witjira today is still a mecca for wildlife. Most of the reeds and large pools of water are gone but 60 springs are still active in the rolling landscape. Picturesque date palms planted by Afghan camel drivers over a hundred years ago dot the area.

Spread over about 70 square kilometres (27 square miles), some springs are mere seepages, dribbles of mineral-rich water. Looking like miniature bleached craters, bubbling pools of warm water lie in their centres surrounded by reeds and other semi-aquatic plants. Pond temperatures range from 30° to 46° C (86–115° F) with the largest and hottest still gushing out half a million litres of water per hour.

The pools themselves are beautiful living systems and because of their isolation from each other, contain numerous endemic species of invertebrates. Three species of fish, including the endemic Dalhousie Hardyhead living in the large permanent ponds, provide a biological puzzle, for no permanent rivers have flowed anywhere near the springs for millions of years.

Wildlife about the Dalhousie Area

Over 50 species of birds have been recorded in the springs area. These include the Sacred and Straw-necked ibis, picking their way through the muddy verge as they dig for worms and mussels with their long curved beaks, the threatened Australian Bustard and the secretive Plains Wanderer. Three species of chats will make a sudden appearance following rain, fluttering like giant

NORTHERN TERRITORY

Abminga R.

Abminga

Mount Dare

OLD GHAN RAIL ROUTE

Spring Ck

Dalhousie Springs

Witjira National Park

N

Hamilton

Adelaide

To Oodnadatta

Location: 280 km (174 miles) east of the Stuart Hwy, extending south of the Northern Territory border to 186 km (116 miles) north of Oodnadatta.

Climate: Desert; extreme summer temperatures 50+° C (122+° F), extremely low humidity. Warm, clear winter days; cool to cold nights. Rain is a rarity, average annual rainfall 150 mm (6 inches).

When to Go: Never in summer; the extreme heat can be deadly. April to September is safe and pleasant.

Access: By unsealed road from Coober Pedy or Marla on Stuart Hwy to Oodnadatta (last fuel), Hamilton and Dalhousie Springs; or unsealed road from Kulgera on Stuart Hwy to Finke, Charlotte Waters, Mount Dare (last fuel) and Dalhousie Springs. Don't travel west from Queensland, steep dunes are impassable. Use 4WD for safety.

Permits: Essential Desert Pass Permit from parks service at Hawker. This includes the Desert Parks Handbook with latest track notes, maps and information. Itinerary must be left with parks service at Hawker for safety.

Equipment: Carry water at *all* times; drive a reliable 4WD with surplus fuel, spare parts and knowledge of car and desert driving. Flying Doctor transceiver equipment, GPS, camping gear, light clothing, strong shoes or boots, hat, sunscreen, full first-aid kit, insect repellent, binoculars, detailed maps, swags.

Facilities: Campsites and 4WD tracks, ranger service, ranger radio network. Fuel at Mt Dare and Oodnadatta, some accommodation and an airstrip at Mt Dare. Camping areas with facilities are planned.

Watching Wildlife: The waters at sunrise and dusk attract birds and mammals. Waterfowl on spring-fed ponds. Dingoes, Red Kangaroos, Euros and eagles almost anytime; reptiles including Perenties and Thorny Devils in autumn and spring.

Visitor Activities: Nature and Aboriginal culture study, 4WD touring, camping, walking.

Above: *Tablelands, red lag gravels glistening with desert varnish, and Spinifex Grass are Witjira's most common features.*

Right: *The park's Dalhousie Springs are a base for excursions into the desert.*

Below: *The Perentie,* Varanus giganteus, *is the world's second-largest lizard.*

butterflies about the gibber plains and shrublands. Along the desert tracks dusky brown Australian Pratincoles sweep into the air on long, slender wings.

Twenty species of native mammals make the park their home although most live out their lives beautifully adapted to a nocturnal and mainly underground life away from the springs. Tiny tracks in the sand are all most visitors will see of these elusive creatures. Incomplete studies in Witjira have brought to light 36 species of reptiles from the giant Perentie varanid, two-and-a-half metres (8 feet) long and often seen hunting about rabbit warrens, to tiny geckoes and skinks.

Witjira Survives

Witjira is the local Aboriginal name for the Tea Trees that overhang Dalhousie Springs. When the overlanders stumbled across these springs in 1870 they found widespread evidence of Aboriginal occupation. European diseases devastated the local people and the destruction of desert springs by cattle broke their seasonal patterns of movement across the land. Today, traditional Aboriginal owners assist parks staff with park management and interpretation, taking special care of sites of Aboriginal significance.

The combination of hard-hoofed, hungry sheep and cattle from the area's early pastoral leases, and feral horses, donkeys and camels has seriously depleted this fragile country, which used to support one soft-footed Red Kangaroo per five square kilometres (1.9 square miles). The land is now making a very slow recovery under its new status as a wilderness national park.

Above: *After rain, claypans fill with sweet water triggering the life cycle of the Shield Shrimp.*

Left: *Most of the lakes in Witjira and out in the Simpson Desert are little more than shallow pans of white salt glistening in the blazing sun.*

WESTERN AUSTRALIA

Covering 2,525,500 square kilometres (974,843 square miles) or around a third of Australia, Western Australia is by far the largest of the country's eight States and Territories. This huge State stretches west of Longitude 129° E to the Indian Ocean and spans a range of climates from the monsoonal Kimberley in the tropical north, through the vast arid inland to the temperate south-west.

While most of Western Australia is flat, there are, broadly speaking, three mountainous areas. The folded ranges of the Kimberley in the north rise to 980 metres (3,214 feet). Cut by deep valleys and gorges, the range of habitats is large and wildlife diversity high. Rivers in the Kimberley become raging flooded torrents in the monsoonal wet season, in contrast to the short coastal rivers south of the Murchison River. On the eastern edge of the Kimberley, Purnululu National Park protects a breathtaking area of brilliantly striped beehive-shaped hills.

To the south, the Pilbara/Hamersley lands encompass the highest mountain in the State (Mt Meharry 1,251 metres/4,103 feet) with broad plateaux cut by deep, narrow gorges, such as those in Karijini National Park. The third region, in the south and south-west, includes some of the oldest (Archaean) rocks on the Earth's surface.

The coastline of 12,500 kilometres (7,763 miles) is highly varied. In the north, the Kimberley coast is deeply indented, rugged and mountainous. Further south, the longest beaches of the continent give way to 2,000 kilometres (1,242 miles) of low, calcareous coastline which includes the vast semi-enclosed waters of the Shark Bay World Heritage Area and the spectacular Zuytdorp cliffs. Extensive seagrass beds in the shallow bay form the perfect habitat for the endangered Dugong.

The high-energy south-west and southern coast is different again, with a spectacular archipelago and granite headlands leading to the 'whale-watching' coast of Fitzgerald National Park and World Biosphere Reserve – habitat for over half the State's wildflower species. Western Australia's famous flora is quite distinct from the flora of eastern Australia as the two are separated by a broad belt of desert.

FITZGERALD RIVER NATIONAL PARK

A Plant Wonderland

Fitzgerald River National Park lies along the southern coast of Western Australia, stretching west for 95 kilometres from near Hopetoun to 180 kilometres east of Albany, an old whaling town. An extensive sandy plain covered mainly by heathland broken by belts of woodland forms the core of the 3,290-square-kilometre (1,270-square mile) park. Four river systems – the West, Fitzgerald, Hamersley, and Gairdner – cut deep valleys through the park's dry sclerophyll wooded uplands before meandering across the plain and slicing through the Barrens. This rugged range of steeply dipping quartzite stretches the length of the seaboard, rising to 500 metres above the plain. Along the coast, a series of quiet lagoons and white sandy beaches at the heads of bays and across estuaries are punctuated by dramatic rocky headlands.

Amidst the magnificent scenery, 20 per cent of Western Australia's extraordinary flora is found in this park, which covers just 0.2 per cent of the State. The importance of the area was first recognized in 1954 when 2,900 square kilometres (1119 square miles) was proclaimed a Reserve for the Preservation of Flora and Fauna. Five years after being given full status as a

Opposite: *The Drummond Track leads across the wide floriferous heathlands of Fitzgerald River National Park.*

Above right: *One-sided Bottlebrush,* Calothamnus sp.

Previous pages

P130: *A yacht sails by the Peron Peninsula which separates the shallow bays of the Shark Bay World Heritage Area.*
P131: *The Red and Green Kangaroo Paw,* Anigozanthos manglesii, *is the floral emblem of Western Australia.*

national park in 1973, Fitzgerald River was declared a World Biosphere Reserve – acknowledging the supreme botanical importance of this floriferous park.

Why so Many Wildflowers?

The dramatic and varied landscape of Fitzgerald River National Park also happens to lie across rapidly declining rainfall gradients, both from west to east and from the ocean inland. Combine a very complex soils mosaic and the widely changing climates of the past million years with extremely varied relief, aspect and rainfall, and the result is an incredibly rich array of flora.

Of the 1,800 plant species found in the park, at least 75 are endemic to the park and a further 50 are endemic to the region. The rarity of many of the plants and the threat posed by collection and harvesting, as well as the destruction of habitat outside the park, has seen Fitzgerald River recognized as the most important flora conservation reserve in south-western Australia by both State and Federal governments.

Flower Walks

July to November produces the most spectacular burst of wildflowers. Hamersley Drive leads to a number of wildflower walks including the West Beach, Mylies Beach and East Mount Barren walks, though the roadside itself provides the best cross section of flora.

The acacias flower first, their bright yellow puffballs covering the slopes, then the unusual kangaroo paws, the fiery Royal Hakeas and eucalypts, particularly the mallees. Many of the 208 species of the Myrtaceae family in the park, particularly the eucalypts, flower in summer. Orchids flower best after bushfires and from June

Map labels
South Coast Hwy
To Esperance
To Albany
Ranger Station
Hamersley R.
Fitzgerald River National Park
Fitzgerald R.
Hopetoun
SOUTHERN OCEAN
N
Perth
Bremer Bay

Location: South coast of Western Australia, 187 km (116 miles) east of Albany via Mount Maxwell and 246 km (153 miles) west of Esperance via Hopetoun.

Climate: Mediterranean climate; cool, damp and windy winters; hot, dry summers with periods dominated by arid, northerly winds.

When to Go: For wildflowers, July–December, peaking in spring; summer on the beaches and inlets; whale watching, August-November.

Access: Various roads off Hwy 1. Coach from Albany and Esperance.

Permits: Camping permit available from rangers or parks offices; access to some mountains is closed to control the spread of root rot or 'dieback', prevalent throughout south-west Australia.

Equipment: Car-camping gear, water, maps, fishing gear, strong walking shoes, hat, sunscreen, insect repellent, weatherproof clothing in winter, binoculars for whale watching, light clothing in summer.

Facilities: Walking tracks, 4WD and 2WD access roads. Vehicle-based camping areas at Four Mile Beach, and at Hamersley, Fitzgerald and Saint Marys inlets, Quoin Head/Whalebone Bay, free gas cooking. Park water supplies are very limited so bring bottled water. Ranger services and four visitor information stations.

Watching Wildlife: Whale watching is best August-November. Nectar-seeking wildlife prolific when the wildflowers are blooming. Reptiles, including some venomous species, are common in spring (if it's warm), early summer and autumn. The park also has some unusual brackish-water frogs. Ospreys can be spotted along the coast.

Visitor Activities: Walking, camping, studying flora, fishing, birdwatching.

December 1989, one summer fire burned 48 per cent (1,570 square kilometres/606 square miles) of this very large park. Researchers working on the park's permanent study transects found that one tiny transect with 23 species growing on it before the fire had a remarkable 45 species growing on it one year after the fire.

Banksias, hakeas and many other proteaceous species protect seeds inside hard woody pods, capsules or shells. These require drying through roasting to free the seeds or to allow water into the seed.

Other species produce vast numbers of long-lived seed stimulated to grow by a clear-burnt ground surface covered with an ash bed rich in nutrients. Many species shoot from buds buried in root stocks safe below the ground and a number of mallee eucalypts are triggered to shoot from lignotubers (woody tubers) when their leaves are scorched and burned. There is even evidence that gases released by fire can stimulate growth and flowering in orchids, Grasstrees and Kangaroo Paws.

Beyond Flowers

Of the many walks in the park, the most rewarding are the East Mount Barren track, near the Hopetoun entrance to the park, the Point Ann Heritage Trail, near the mouth of the Fitzgerald River, and the spectacular Whalebone Bay to Quoin Head track where whale sightings are a certainty during winter and spring.

Above: *Humpback Whales,* Megaptera novaeangliae, *can be seen breaching off the park coastline.*

Right: *Spreading Rick Rack or Showy Banksia,* Banksia speciosa, *grows on sandy country and reaches a height of 5 metres (16 feet).*

to August. About a hundred species of orchids and nine hybrids are now known from Fitzgerald River National Park, many of which occur nowhere else in the world.

The coastal Barrens seem to have formed a refuge through time for species adapted to a temperate climate such as Banksias and Lambertias as well as some of the parks 200 species of legumes. The East Mount Barren walk winds for kilometres through shrublands carrying 82 species of epacrids – tough spiky shrubs that bear bright white or pink tubular flowers rich in nectar.

Miracle of the Phoenix Plants

Bushfires from lightning strikes are part of the natural park environment and, while a change in the intensity and regularity of fires could exhaust the seed supply, many Australian plants require fire to flower. In

Several 2WD and 4WD roads provide access to key areas. Quiss Road, in the western half of the park, leads to Point Anne – a spectacular vantage point offering magnificent views up and down the coast. Between August and November this is a good spot to keep an eye out for Humpback and Southern Right whales as they migrate from the Southern Ocean up the West Australian coast to the Shark Bay area. While the water is chilly in winter, the pristine white sand beaches of the park are glorious all year round and there are plenty of places to swim and to fish.

The south-west of Australia is seriously infected by a fungal root-rotting disease commonly known as 'dieback' which can wipe out thousands of hectares of vegetation. Fitzgerald River National Park is possibly the least affected area, so off-road driving is strictly prohibited and the bottoms of cars, tyres and footwear should be washed before entering the park.

Top: *Quoin Head is one of the best spots in the park for whale watching.*

Left: *The Spider Orchid,* Caladenia patersonii, *grows in the understorey of coastal shrub and heath.*

KALBARRI NATIONAL PARK

Murchison Gorge and Heathlands

Established in 1963, Kalbarri is one of Western Australia's most diverse parks – a gently undulating landscape of dry sandy soils slashed by the spectacular serpentine gorge of the Murchison River. Smaller gorges cut by lesser streams shape the rugged coastline. Mallee and heath cover the gently sloping plateau top, by far the largest plant communities in the park, while the gorge sides and floor, which varies from a few metres (10 feet) wide to half a kilometre (1,640 feet), is wooded with paperbarks, River Red Gums and acacias. From late July, wildflowers bloom across the sandy heathland that covers much of the park's 1,830-square kilometres 706-square mile).

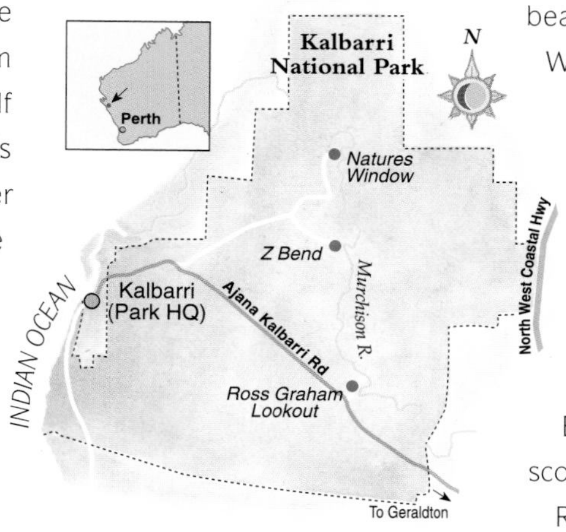

Of all the West Australian parks, Kalbarri has perhaps the most amenable year-round climate. This subtropical and semi-arid park is located 590 kilometres north of Perth. As the park is coastal, winter and summer temperatures are moderated by the sea.

A Gorgeous Place

The magnificent Murchison Gorge is one of the main attractions of Kalbarri National Park. With dramatic red sandstone walls, in many places towering 200 metres (656 feet) above the river, the gorge winds its way for 90 kilometres (56 miles) to the sea. Canoe tours and treks

Opposite: Steps and a track lead down from the lookout at Z Bend through the red sandstone of Murchison Gorge.

Above right: The Great Egret, Ardea alba, fishes the shallows of the Murchison with White-faced and Pacific herons.

along the gorge can be organized from the town of Kalbarri, at the mouth of the Murchison River, but there is plenty of opportunity for independent exploration.

An almost circular entrenched meander known as The Loop, 26 kilometres down an access gravel road from the main Kalbarri road, presents a wonderful introduction to the gorge. A walking track around this beautiful meander begins at Nature's Window at the end of the access road. This unusual 'window' was formed when the underlying layers of a massive sandstone slab were eroded away. Some of these fossil-bearing layers reveal ancient sand ripples, others are dotted with the tracks of long-dead animals, particularly Eurypterids, which resemble immense scorpions, and wormholes.

River Red Gums and paperbark trees line the pools of The Loop. Great Egrets stand by the edge, reflected in the still water of wonderful swimming holes, while rock wallabies along the cliffed terraces and Euros on the rocky screes rest up in the shade. Z Bend lookout, the other main destination at the end of the Loop access track, provides the most spectacular views into the Murchison River, although the views from Hawks Head and Ross Graham Lookout further inland are also very beautiful in a dramatic way.

Sandplain heath

The dry sandy coastal soils of southern Australia, deficient in phosphates and trace elements, usually produce a heathland of immense botanical variety. With over 600 flowering species, the Kalbarri moors are no exception.

A visitor driving along any of the park roads from July to September witnesses a spectacular flowering succession. The yellow-gold of the acacias sweeps across the

(Map labels: Kalbarri National Park; Perth; INDIAN OCEAN; Natures Window; Z Bend; Kalbarri (Park HQ); Ajana Kalbarri Rd; Murchison R.; North West Coastal Hwy; Ross Graham Lookout; To Geraldton; N)

Location: At the mouth of the Murchison River, 590 km (366 miles) north of Perth and 168 km (104 miles) from Geraldton.

Climate: Four seasons; summer temperatures reach 40° C (104° F), low humidity and often windy; winter ranges from 10°–20° C (50–68° F) with most rain June and July.

When to Go: Any time. Best wildflowers August to end September; honeyeaters and migratory waders, August–November. Most comfortable temperatures and humidity, April–May, August–October.

Access: By road from Highway 1 and Ajana to Kalbarri road. By air to Geraldton where car hire is available. Gravel park roads to the gorge lookouts; coast access from the Kalbarri to Balline road.

Permits: Visitor entry fee from Kalbarri tourist centre or park entry station coin machine. See ranger for special rules for canoeing and hiking the Murchison Gorge.

Equipment: Drinking water, first-aid kit, insect repellent, sunscreen 30+ SPF, broad-brimmed hat, strong walking shoes, canoe, light summer clothing, warm winter wear and waterproof jacket, binoculars, wildflower field guide.

Facilities: Ranger services, four picnic areas and toilets (free gas barbecues only at Nature's Window and Z Bend), walking trails, self-guided nature trail at Mushroom Rock. Kalbarri has a full range of accommodation available.

Watching Wildlife: Honeyeaters amongst the wildflowers, late July to late September; migratory birds, October through summer; waterbirds on the river, spring to autumn; reptiles, August–April.

Visitor Activities: Nature studies including botany, ornithology, geology and geomorphology. Walking, canoeing wild river after rain.

Right: *The road to this dramatic lookout at The Loop on Murchison Gorge crosses many kilometres of flowering heathland.*

Above: *The Thorny Devil, Moloch horridus, is an inoffensive ant-eating dragon lizard which lives in hot sandy country.*

Far right: *The Western Grey Kangaroo is found throughout Australia and can be identified by the white flashes in its ears.*

land joined by the paler orange-yellow of banksias, grevilleas and dryandras. Other deep red grevilleas and hakeas combine with the deep yellow of the irises, geebungs and delicate waxy *Diuris* orchids. Crimson and pink flickers throughout the bush in the stiffly erect *Verticordias*, the bottlebrushes and graceful wax plants as well as the nobbly *Isopogons* and starry Turkey Bush.

Grasstrees, a symbol of these heaths, shoot creamy spikes three metres (10 feet) into the air from mops of stiff green grass-like leaves on thick fire-blackened trunks. Fringed Lilies, Tinsel Lilies and *Hoveas* bring deep blues and purples to the spectrum of colours, while the unusual Kangaroo Paws and Cats Paws – so named because the individual flowers look like tiny fuzzy animal paws – range from an alarming black to crimson and green.

Creatures of the Heath

The flowers of the heathland are a honeypot for birds. Singing, White-plumed and Brown honeyeaters, Purple-crowned Lorikeets and Red Wattle Birds are among the thousands of nectar-lovers hovering about from July to September or until the flowering bonanza finishes.

Stalking through the heath the giant flightless Emu devours soft fruits, seeds and insects, even small birds and mammal carrion. The Emu plays a significant role in the germination processes of some plants by partly digesting impervious seed covers then delivering the seed in a splat of fertilizer to the sandy soil surface. The deep green eggs of this unusual bird are about the size of a mini football and the chicks, unlike their parents, are beautifully striped.

Sheltering in thickets of mallee eucalypts, Grasstrees and thicker scrub, families of Western Grey Kangaroos wait for late afternoon to begin their grazing and to move towards the river and other watering points. Twelve species of native mammals have been recorded in the park, but most are nocturnal and difficult to spot.

SHARK BAY WORLD HERITAGE AREA

A Priceless Nursery

Shark Bay World Heritage Area encompasses 23,000 square kilometres (8,878 square miles) of sweeping coast and aquamarine seas around Australia's westernmost point. The warm waters bathe rich marine habitats supporting an incredible diversity of life including dolphins, Dugong, great rays, sharks, octopus and many visiting Humpback Whales. Shark Bay is also an important nursery ground for countless larval crustaceans, molluscs and fishes.

The boundary of the World Heritage Area follows the coast north from Hamelin Pool to Carnarvon for 190 kilometres (118 miles) then shoots out to sea and angles south to enclose the Bernier, Dorre and Dirk Hartog islands and the Zuytdorp Cliffs within an area three nautical miles from the coast before continuing back to Hamelin Pool. This prodigious area includes the Shark Bay Marine Protected Area, the Francois Peron National Park and numerous island nature reserves. Listed in 1991, Shark Bay and surrounds was one of the few places on the planet to fulfil all four World Heritage criteria of 'outstanding natural universal values'.

Warm, Shallow Seas

The warm shallow waters of Shark Bay shelter over 4,000 square kilometres (1,544 square miles) of seagrass. Twelve separate species make this the most diverse seagrass community in the world – paradise for an estimated 10,000 Dugong and 6,000 marine turtles. The turtle population includes the increasingly rare

Above right: Masses of tiny bleached shells form beaches and high ridges at Shell Bay in the World Heritage Area.

Loggerhead Turtle. Somewhere between 10 and 30 of these animals nest on the beaches of Dirk Hartog Island each night of the early summer breeding season.

For the half-tonne Dugong, Shark Bay is probably the most significant nursery area in tropical Australian waters, if not the world. Safe from hunting and harassment for many years, the Dugong in the bay have become so inquisitive that they can be readily photographed underwater. Friendly Bottle-nosed Dolphins are also common, with a pod visiting Monkey Mia each morning and afternoon.

An unusual product of the hypersaline waters of Hamelin Pool are the so-called 'living dinosaurs' or stromatolites, resembling lumps of rock beneath the water. Part living organism, part inanimate sand, they are a bizarre reminder of life on Earth around 3,500 million years ago.

Island and Mainland Life

Six thousand years ago the sea reached its present level and the islands of Shark Bay, with their stunted scrubby vegetation and shrubland wildlife habitats, were cut off from the mainland. Today, many species ravaged to extinction on the mainland by feral animals survive on the islands. Of the 26 species of endangered Australian mammals, five are found only on Bernier and Dorre islands – the Burrowing Bettong, Rufous Hare Wallaby, Banded Hare Wallaby, Shark Bay Mouse and the Western Barred Bandicoot.

Birds were less affected by the feral invasion and today 230 species have been recorded in the area. Magnificent Brahmany Kites, Ospreys and White-bellied Sea Eagles sweep effortlessly above the shorelines, while

Location: 833 km (517 miles) north of Perth, Shark Bay World Heritage Area straddles Latitude 26° S.

Climate: Mild to hot, from 25° C (77° F) in winter to 33° C (91° F) in summer. Rainfall irregular, from 200–400 mm (7 5/8–15 3/4 inches) annually. Possible summer cyclones.

When to Go: Anytime, climate most comfortable April–September; wildflowers seen 6–8 weeks after rain. Migratory waders October–April.

Access: All-weather sealed road to Denham and Monkey Mia, good gravel to Hamelin and Useless Loop. 4WD tracks to key areas of park. Bus to Overlander Roadhouse, Denham and Carnarvon. By air to Carnarvon. Numerous boat ramps.

Permits: Pay entrance fees at honesty box near Peron Homestead or parks office, Denham. Permission needed to enter private areas.

Equipment: 4WD vehicle, fuel, spares, tyre pump and gauge. Fishing gear, swimming gear, light clothing, insect repellent, sunscreen 30+ SPF, broad-brimmed hat, water (none available on Peron Peninsula), binoculars, strong sandshoes, fuel stove and fuel. Boating gear should include HF or VHF radio, flares, lifejackets, tide and marine charts.

Facilities: 4WD tracks, primitive campsites Herald Bight, Gregories, Big Lagoon and Steep Point; interpreted and self-guided tracks; artesian bath at Peron Homestead. Accommodation at Denham, Monkey Mia, Carnarvon, Nanga Homestead; light plane hire at Denham.

Watching Wildlife: Humpback Whales in bays, dolphins at Monkey Mia; dugongs on the seagrass beds; migratory waders October–April; pelicans any time. Aerial observation of large sea animals.

Visitor Activities: Boating, fishing, swimming, whale watching, dolphin interaction, walking, birdwatching, camping, nature study.

nesting colonies of Wedge-tailed Shearwaters and Sooty Terns find a safe haven on Shark Bay's many islands.

Nearly 100 species of reptiles and amphibians in the area include three endemic sand-swimming skinks and 10 of the 30 Australian dragons. Brightly coloured seasnakes (docile and inquisitive in the water but highly venomous) can be spotted from time to time in the shallows and are sometimes washed up amongst seaweed.

Boat tours of the area are available from Denham and Monkey Mia, small settlements within Shark Bay, but only an overflight can reveal the spectacular juxtaposition of land and sea. Unimaginable blues slide into white beaches and coppery red sand dunes. The mighty waves of the Indian Ocean are tamed against the Zuytdorp Cliffs, a 100-kilometre (62-mile) 'breakwater' for Shark Bay.

Left: *The Zuytdorp Cliffs were named after a Dutch ship wrecked on its run to the 'Spice Islands' of Indonesia.*

Above: *Wedge-tailed Shearwaters,* Puffinus pacificus, *are commonly seen as rafts of dark birds floating on the sea.*

Below: *Loggerhead Turtle hatchlings run the gauntlet of crabs and seabirds as they cross a beach at Turtle Bay.*

Return of the Native

A remarkable vermin-proof fence has been constructed across the narrow neck of the Peron Peninsula near Shell Beach. Once the fence was securely in place, all foxes were removed from the peninsula and some of the native species once restricted to the safety of the islands in the area were released there. As vehicles cross the road grid at the only gap in the fence, a momentarily mysterious loud dog barking is heard. Breaking an infra-red beam triggers a recording which, together with the grid and the fence, appears to deter foxes quite effectively.

In another move to recolonize Western Australia with animals now extinct in the State, 40 Great Stick Nest Rats from a successful breeding program in South Australia were released on Salutation Island. Once common across southern inland Australia, this gentle and beautiful animal now has a chance to increase its range.

Top: *The spectacular semi-arid Peron Peninsula National Park is one of the reserves within the world heritage area.*

Above left: *Playful Bottle-nosed Dolphins are often seen in Shark Bay – some meet visitors daily at Monkey Mia beach.*

Above right: *Around 10 per cent (10,000) of the world's remaining Dugongs graze the seagrass beds of Shark Bay.*

KARIJINI NATIONAL PARK

The Hamersley Iron-rich Gorge Country

Hamersley Range National Park, proclaimed in 1980, was recently renamed Karijini in recognition of the continuing significance of this spectacular gorge country to the Panyjima, Innawonga and Kurrama Aboriginal people. Karijini is now one of many national parks in Australia run jointly by the parks service and the local Aboriginal people, who contribute a deep knowledge and understanding of their land to park management.

Lying in the heart of the wild Pilbara region of Western Australia, the park stretches across part of a massive block of weathered iron-rich rock 450 kilometres (279 miles) long. At 6,275 square kilometres (2,422 miles), it is the second largest national park in Western Australia.

Millions of years ago this landscape was buckled, crushed and folded by immense mountain-building forces. Later, water draining from the heights followed the joints and faults, opening them up into the wonderful gorges and bold red, stepped landscapes typical of Karijini today. The Fortescue River, a mighty torrent in the summer wet season, drains all five of the area's great gorges.

The park is located off the Great Northern Highway 285 kilometres (177 miles) from Port Hedland and 180 kilometres (112 miles) from Newman. Karijini protects a large section of land in an area otherwise heavily mined for iron ore. The Pilbara contains the world's largest iron mines at Tom Price, Newman and Paraburdoo.

Opposite: *Fortescue Falls and plunge pool is one of the many perfect swimming holes in the Karijini National Park.*

Above right: *The Desert Bloodwood, Eucalyptus terminalis, produces masses of creamy flowers in July after rain.*

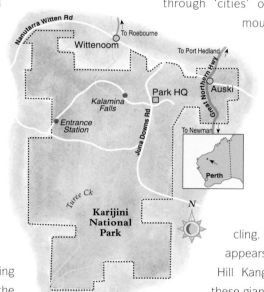

Dry season deserts

During the dry season, the park's rolling hills are covered with blonde Spinifex Grass hummocks and occasional bare patches of deep red lateritic soils. Scattered stands of Snappy Gum, looking very much like the less common Ghost Gum, shine bright white against the iron-rich land. The excellent gravel roads of the park regularly pass through 'cities' of reddish chocolate termite mounds, ranging from one to four metres (3–13 feet) in height.

Termites play a critical role throughout the Spinifex country. They cut the hard dry Spinifex leaves into short lengths, which they then store in the mound's cells before consuming them and converting these extremely tough leaves into nutrients for recycling. The only other animal that appears to eat Spinifex is the Euro, or Hill Kangaroo. Richer than chocolate, these giant mounds are also small worlds that house not only termites but dragons, geckoes, pardalotes (small finch-like birds) and other beasts, even the Dingo – Australia's native dog. Even Australian Kestrels and Grey Falcons use some of the towering skyscrapers as lookouts to spy for their prey.

Deep, cool gorges

Even in the winter dry season, days are mostly very warm so visitors usually focus on the five gorges which drain northwards as tributaries of the Fortescue River—Dales, Yampire, Kalamina, Wittenoom (which breaks into a knot of five in its upper reaches) and Hamersley. Standing on the narrow razorback ridge at Oxer Lookout, 300 metres (984 feet) above the confluence of the five gorges of the Wittenoom group, is absolutely spellbinding if not terrifying. Fig trees overhanging the chasm clutch narrow ledges. Pockets of papery-petalled

Location: In the Pilbara district of Western Australia, at the headwaters of the Fortescue River, on the Great Northern Highway 285 km (177 miles) from Port Hedland.

Climate: Dry tropical, two seasons. The park experiences an unreliable wet season from December–April, average maximum temperature 37° C (97° F), high humidity, intense rain depressions. Very reliable dry season, June–November, average maximum temperature 30° C (86° F), extremely low humidity. Coolest from June–August. July minimum temperature 12° C (54° F).

When to Go: May–September (not summer). Best wildflowers seen six weeks after major rains. Wildlife at waterholes July–November.

Access: By car or coach on good roads from Roebourne, Port Hedland and Newman. Beware road closures in wet season. By air from Perth to Newman, Paraburdoo and Port Hedland.

Permits: Pay camping fees at national parks office, Karratha, or at park ranger station. Inform ranger if planning major gorge walks.

Equipment: Broad-brimmed hat, sunscreen 30+ SPF, fly veil, light daytime clothing, warm evening wear; first-aid kit, strong walking shoes or boots, binoculars, camping gear and fuel stove, swimming gear, car tools and spares. Carry water in car and on walks – take four litres per person per day.

Facilities: The camping areas at Dales Gorge, Weano Gorge and Joffre Intersection have gas barbecues and pit toilets. Drinking water is available at Dales Turnoff and 3 kilometres (almost 2 miles) west of Joffre camp. Excellent brochure describes tracks.

Watching Wildlife: Wildlife by waterholes in the dry season.

Visitor Activities: Wildlife study and birdwatching, camping, swimming, walking, gorge scrambles. Note: Lower Yampire and Wittenoom Gorge dust carries dangerous blue asbestos particles.

Golden Everlastings cling to the precipice, as do stark white Snappy Gums – perches for Peregrine Falcons and Wedge-tailed Eagles. Emu Bushes and the Caustic Vine – a leafless plant with caustic milky sap and a tangled knot of pencil-thick green stems doubling as leaves – share the dry upper stepped walls with the ubiquitous Spinifex.

Life Around the Pools

The climb down the track to Fortescue Falls at the end of Dales Gorge provides a good introduction to Karijini gorge bottoms. The falls drop in a diagonal skein across the fine russet rock layers rich in iron. Some of the beautifully smooth and squared layers show the fine cracks that have been filled in later with dark minerals – stunning models for geological study.

The plunge pool is deep and pale green, surrounded with reeds and sedges. Masses of ferns, spikerushes, Milfoil, Swamp Lily, *Vallisneria*, Nardoo and other aquatic plants live in the stream beyond the pool. In seepage water weeping down the gorge walls, Maiden Hair ferns with multi-fingered leaves thrive in the shade of cajeputs (paperbarks) and sturdy River Red Gums. Dragonfly nymphs are very common in the waters with large numbers of red, blue, brown and gold adults hovering about the pools and resting.

Slow-moving waters inside the gorges are usually quite cold but warmer unshaded pools in wider parts of the gorges are extremely rich with plant and invertebrate life. Larger animals, such as kangaroos, and countless numbers of birds can be seen around the downstream pools

Right: *Hamersley Gorge is more accessible than other gorges in Karijini NP.*

Below: *Handrail Pool provides cool relief and stunning colours as a reward for the climb down into narrow Weano Gorge.*

just inside the ranges before the gorges open out into the broad Fortescue River valley. Karijini is also home to at least 128 bird species and these pools attract thousands of Corellas and Galahs as well as Red-tailed Black Cockatoos, Spinifex Pigeons and countless smaller birds, particularly Budgerigars and Zebra Finches.

Indigenous know-how

After tens of thousands of years in occupation, Aboriginal peoples across Australia have developed an incredibly rich understanding of the way the seasons cycle, how the ecosystems function, where the plants and animals are and how they interact. At Karijini, the people lived on the land like people on a large outback property. They had fixed camps for special times of the year; when they moved camp to another place on their land, they had reason to do so and could predict what the conditions would be. Today, that knowledge and understanding contributes to Karijini's management program. It is hoped that the two Aboriginal rangers now working in the park, through cooperation with the Karijini Aboriginal Corporation, will be the first of many.

Right: *A desert monitor,* Varanus gouldii gouldii.

Below: *Wildflowers carpet the ground soon after summer storms or autumn rains at Karijini National Park.*

Above: *Blue skies, Spinifex Grass, Ghost Gums and glowing red cliffs epitomise Karijini in winter and spring.*

Overleaf: *Ancient layers of iron-impregnated sandstone can be seen across the yawning Red Gorge from Oxers Lookout.*

Purnululu (Bungle Bungle) National Park

The Awesome Bungle Bungle Beehives

Purnululu, one of Australia's greatest natural wonders, is so remote it was known only by local Aboriginal people and some pastoralists until it was 'discovered' by a passing film crew in the early 1980s. Located in the wild tropical north of Western Australia on the eastern edge of the remote Kimberley region, the park is 109 kilometres north of Halls Creek and 250 kilometres south of Kununurra.

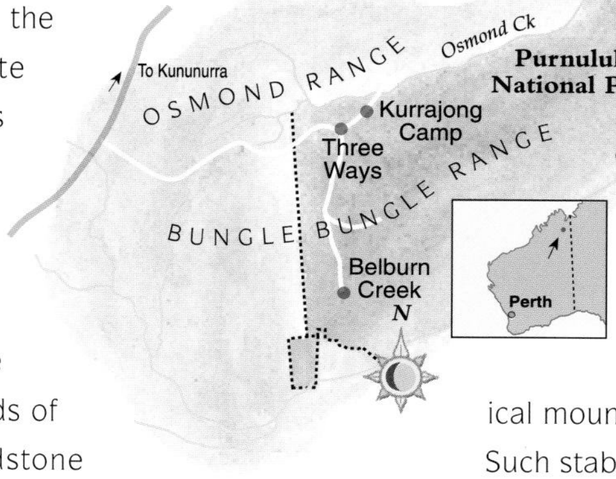

Three thousand square kilometres (1,158 square miles) of park enclose hundreds of conical towers of sandstone 200–300 metres (656-984 feet) high, all with exquisite thin, horizontal orange and sooty layers. Streams draining off the towers and an internal plateau alternate between raging torrents in the wet season and falls of white sand between chains of waterholes in the dry. The park was proclaimed a Nature Reserve in 1987 and later converted to National Park status.

Cones and stripes

Millions of years ago, large rivers ran from ranges to the north-west sweeping sand and gravels into Purnululu's Ord Basin. Layers of pebbles were followed by layers of sand and mud until uplifting halted the process. Ever

Opposite: *Purnululu National Park's famous clusters of banded sandstone 'beehives' are spectacular from the air.*

Above right: *Nimble Ring-tailed Dragons,* Cienophorus caudicinctus, *reach up to 30 centimetres (12 inches).*

since the continent drifted into the tropics, intense rainfall in the wet season from November to April has washed away the 'cement' which normally fills the gaps between particles in the sandstone. This has left the rock vulnerable to even light knocks, but still immensely strong when compressed. Over millions of years the wild waters have carved spectacular narrow gorges and vast undercut galleries – such as Cathedral Gorge and Echidna Chasm – while the conical mounds in between remain stable.

Such stability is partly the result of the distinctive striped surface of the mounds. This thin protective skin is, in fact, only a few millimetres (a quarter of an inch) thick and covers the original soft white sandstone underneath. The sooty black is organic material while the orange is clay and silica. Even this protective coat is extremely fragile and breaking off a small piece can lead to extensive erosion of the soft underlying sandstone.

A Bungle Bungle Overview

Because road access is limited to 4WD vehicles, the majority of visitors see these wilderness mountains from the air—a truly spectacular sight. Flying from Kununurra or Halls Creek, light aircraft run three trips each day and helicopter flights are also available within the park. In the rippling oppressive heat of the dry and early wet seasons, the complex pattern of 'beehives', gorges and streams spreads out below in a breathtaking tableau. In the wet season, stormy skies with massive thunderheads rumble darkly over the full glory of torrential waterfalls,

Location: In the eastern Kimberley, 250 km (155 miles) south of Kununurra and 47 km (29 miles) from Highway 1.

Climate: Tropical, two seasons. Wet season December–April, average maximum temperature 32° C (90° F) high humidity, stormy with intense rain periods and major flooding. Dry season May–October, average maximum temperature 34° C (93° F), very low humidity rising to high in October. Coolest June–August.

When to Go: June–September best for walking; aerial visits anytime; wildflowers, May and June; wildlife, June–September, (wildlife crowds remaining water, August–October).

Access: By road 4WD-only after leaving Hwy 1, no caravans. Helicopter flights from airport near campgrounds.

Permits: Vehicle entrance fee plus camping fee payable at self-registration honesty box at ranger station.

Equipment: 4WD vehicle with ample fuel and appropriate spares and tools, light clothing, broad-brimmed hat, first-aid kit, sunscreen 30+ SPF, insect repellent, fly veil, camping gear, day or overnight pack, waterbottles, binoculars. Make sure you are completely self-sufficient!

Facilities: 4WD tracks, some signage and interpretation leaflets, campsites with water and pit toilets at Walardi and Kurrajong. Ranger, water, shop information centre and toilets near Three Ways; fuel at Turkey Creek on Hwy 1.

Watching Wildlife: Birdlife can be seen by waterholes at sunrise and dusk although seed-eaters can be seen throughout the day, especially parrots, pigeons and finches. Mammals also come to water. Reptiles and invertebrates can be seen at anytime.

Visitor Activities: 4WD-drive touring, helicopter flights, Aboriginal art study, birdwatching, walking.

Map labels: To Kununurra · OSMOND RANGE · Osmond Ck · Purnululu National Park · Kurrajong Camp · Three Ways · BUNGLE BUNGLE RANGE · Ord R. · Belburn Creek · N · Perth

Exploring the Sacred Silence

While there is an airstrip in the park, visitors who wish to explore Purnululu from the ground usually arrive by 4WD and stay at least several days. (Park roads are closed during the wet season from January to April.) Although several longer walks are well-marked and interesting, the short walk from Piccaninny Creek carpark to Cathedral Gorge should not be overlooked.

After an easy but hot tramp amongst clumps of blonde, needle-like Spinifex Grass along the broad walled-in valley of a tributary of Piccaninny Creek, the visitor enters the side of a fantastic dimly lit domed chamber 80 metres (262 feet) deep with a pristine white sand floor. The track leads straight to the very centre where a circular drop pool of water 10 metres (33 feet) across mirrors the opening in the domed roof. The creek falls through this opening during the wet season. There is no sound except the sighing of the wind far above and, somewhere outside, the deep cooing of a White-quilled Rock Pigeon temporarily frightened away from its drinking hole. Deep silence and cooler temperatures evoke the sanctity of this place for the local Kaja people.

A Grand Walk

After Cathedral Gorge, the second 'compulsory' trip is to walk as far up Piccaninny Creek as time allows; it is best to camp up there overnight. Start early while the gorge is bathed in cool, purple light and the majority of the park's 130-plus species of birds can be seen coming to the deep, scattered waterholes for water. Emerald flocks

Right: *The towering golden walls of Cathedral Gorge narrow to an opening through which water gushes in the wet season.*

Below: *Piccaninny Creek has cut a valley through the beehives, giving easy walking access to the interior of the park.*

the tiger-striped mounds glistening in occasional shafts of sunlight. The traditional owners, the Kaja language group, were happiest during the wet and soon after when a fantastic array of vegetable and animal foods meant plenty of time available for ceremonial life.

of Budgerigars, pink and grey Galahs, Red-backed Wrens, Rainbow Bee-eaters, Rock Pigeons and even what the local people call 'turkeys', the Australian Bustard, are all very active in the cool of the morning. Most of all this is the land of tiny finches. The Long-tailed, Star, Crimson, Zebra and that supreme beauty, the Gouldian, finch, all feed out among the dry grassy patches, returning often to water.

Early morning is also the best time to see the Euro and the Northern Nail Tail Wallaby – a macropod with a strange long slender tail ending with a 'thumbnail' of unknown use. Only the very alert will see the small Narbarlek or Short-eared Rock Wallaby high up on the park's rocky ledges. Sharing the ledges and crannies of the beetling red cliffs in the narrowing gorge are many slender fine-leafed Fan Palms and the ubiquitous fig, another relict of ancient rainforested times.

Streaming from the cliff edge far above, a dark lichen stain from a wet season waterfall leads to a plunge pool clustered with mosses, ferns, sedges, acacias and melaleucas. This microcosm of the Piccaninny Creek ecosystem draws grasshoppers, bees, wasps, skinks,

geckoes, dragons, monitors and many more species yet to be described. Soon the walk becomes a rock-hopping exercise in a slot a few metres wide until, 23 kilometres (14.3 miles) from the start, and deep within the Bungle Bungle Ranges, the Piccaninny Gorge ends at a wall.

Above: *Budgerigars,* Melopsittacus undulatus, *take a drink.*

Top: *Purnululu's Piccaninny Creek in flood is an unusual sight – the park is inaccessible in the wet season.*

NORTHERN TERRITORY

From the green tropics of the Top End to the red centre at the heart of Australia, the Northern Territory covers 1,346,200 square kilometres (519,633 square miles) or 17.5 per cent of the continent. The coastline extends for 6,200 kilometres (3,850 miles) across the north, but it is that great lonely red monolith Uluru (Ayers Rock), far to the south in the Uluru–Kata Tjuta National Park, which attracts most visitors to the Territory every year. The park is one of several in Australia co-managed by traditional Aboriginal owners.

Between the extremes of the wet tropics and the Simpson Desert lie a range of interwoven ecosystems. Many of these – tropical eucalypt forest, monsoon rain-forest, mangrove forest, woodland savanna, tropical grassland and shrubland – can be experienced in Kakadu National Park World Heritage Area. Others, such as desert hummock grassland, scrubland and salt lakes are found in the arid south.

The MacDonnell Ranges to the south contain the richest wildlife habitats of arid Australia, including the deep gorges, permanent waterholes and outwash plains of the West MacDonnell National Park. South of the MacDonnells, fields of residual plateaux and mesas extend east towards the Simpson Desert where the longest parallel dune systems in the world can be found. Meandering towards salt Lake Eyre, immense systems of ancient sanded rivers are lined with grand River Red Gums surviving on underground waters. The Territory's active tropical rivers in the north – the Alligator, Goyder, Daly, Victoria and others – carry huge volumes of monsoon season floodwaters towards the Arafura and Timor seas.

With such varied habitats and climatic conditions, Northern Territory wildlife is either very mobile or well adapted to local conditions. Of particular interest are Red Kangaroos, Antilopine Wallaroos and Euros as well as a long list of reptile species, from the tiny, prehistoric-looking Thorny Devil to the second-largest lizard in the world, the 2.5 metre (8 foot) Perentie. In the northern wetlands, waterbirds in their tens of thousands share their habitat with huge Saltwater (Estuarine) Crocodiles.

KAKADU NATIONAL PARK

A Supreme Natural and Cultural Heritage

Spectacular Kakadu National Park stretches from the Van Diemen Gulf in the north to the Arnhem Land Plateau in the south and encompasses a land area of 19,804 square kilometres (7,644 square miles) as well as a marine component of 473 square kilometres (183 miles). The park spreads across the catchments of the Wildman, West Alligator, South Alligator and East Alligator rivers, all of which run north into the gulf.

Kakadu covers large representative samples of almost all of the Northern Territory's tropical habitats, from riverine floodplains to 500 kilometres (311 miles) of rugged escarpment with impressive wet-season waterfalls. Many of the park's diverse species of flora and fauna are yet to be described. Aboriginal art in the park dates back over the past 30,000 years, with an estimated 1,500 major galleries of art recording the greatest continuous artistic achievement anywhere on Earth.

The scientific Alligator Rivers Study of 1973 and the exhaustive Ranger Uranium Environmental Inquiry of 1975 recommended the return of Alligator Rivers lands

Opposite: *Mighty Jim Jim Falls, a mere trickle in the dry season, becomes a raging torrent in the wet season.*

Above right: *The park's Red Lily or Lotus,* Nelumbo nucifera.

Previous pages
P152: *Ubirr Rock's barramundi X-ray pictures were painted with stick brushes and ochre by the local Gagudju people.*
P153: *The darter represents the Territory's vast wetlands.*

to the Aboriginal people, the creation of a Kakadu National Park and a closely controlled mining operation. The park was created in three stages with a final addition in 1991. The park area was also listed as a World Heritage Area in three stages and 13,759 square kilometres (5,311 square miles) have been listed as RAMSAR Wetlands of International Importance. Kakadu shares its eastern boundary with the Arnhem Land Aboriginal Reserve, while its western boundary lies 120 kilometres east of Darwin, the Northern Territory's thriving administrative capital.

The Natural Heritage

Kakadu protects an incredible range of habitats including broad saline and riverine mudflats, belts of beautifully zoned mangroves, estuarine systems with tidal extremes that range up to seven metres (22 feet), freshwater riverine systems, sedgelands, swamp forests, gallery rainforests, sclerophyll forests and savanna, as well as extremely ancient sandstone plateaux and outliers with many micro-habitats from arid to saturated.

Flora and fauna populations in Kakadu are large and diverse with over 1,000 species of plants, more than 50 mammal species, 280 bird, 123 reptile and 77 freshwater fish species and over 10,000 species of insect. Such a rich biodiversity, impossible to describe fully on these few pages, offers visitors a lifetime of fascinating discovery.

Tiny marsupials such as Antechinus and Northern Native Cats (Northern Quolls) share the park with the larger possums, agile Nabarlek wallabies and Antilopine Wallaroos. Dozens of bird species include the regal White-bellied Sea Eagle and the Jabiru, glorious

Location: Extends 210 km (130 miles) inland across the catchment of the South Alligator River from the Van Dieman Gulf to the Arnhem Land Plateau. Western boundary 120 km (74.5 miles) east of Darwin.

Climate: Tropical climate; average summer (January) maximum temperature 34° C (93° F), extremely humid and stormy; average winter (July) maximum 30° C (86° F). Park floods December–April. Hottest days in November; coolest days in July. Nights rarely fall below 20° C (68° F).

When to go: May–October but best in June and July; best for plants, May and June; for waterbirds, July–October; nature study anytime.

Access: By road, bus or car via Arnhem and Kakadu highways. By air, light aircraft to Gagudju Cooinda Lodge and Jabiru. Boat ramps at Cooinda, Jim Jim Creek, Border Store and South Alligator River Crossing.

Permits: Pay park entry fees and camping fees at park entry stations.

Equipment: Light clothing, strong walking shoes or boots, broad-brimmed hat, sunscreen, insect repellent, light rain gear, binoculars. Coolbox for camera and film. Swimming gear for crocodile-free areas, fishing gear, first-aid kit, mosquito-proof camping gear, fuel stove and fuel.

Facilities: Visitor information centre, cultural centre, walking tracks, boat ramps, Aboriginal ranger services, unpowered camping areas, supermarket at Jabiru and essentials at Border Store, accommodation in park, artsite interpretation.

Watching Wildlife: Almost anywhere at anytime, bird hides on Mamukala Floodplain, Yellow Water guided boat tour from Cooinda, Man-Ngarre walk.

Visitor Activities: Birdwatching, nature study, Aboriginal art study, camping, boating, fishing, walking, 4WD touring, swimming.

Above: *The Black-necked Stork or Jabiru struts about the wetlands feeding on fish, snakes and frogs.*

Top right: *The dangerous Saltwater or Estuarine Crocodile grows to seven metres (22 feet).*

Above right: *Yellow Water cruises are fabulous wildlife spotting experiences.*

Right: *Kakadu's Oenpelli Python, Australia's largest, lives in the monsoon forests of the escarpment.*

Gouldian Finches and Red-winged Parrots. Harmless to humans, the large, carnivorous Ghost Bat hunts large insects, frogs, lizards, roosting birds and even other bats.

Kakadu also contains what is probably the largest population of Saltwater (Estuarine) Crocodiles in the world, with some huge beasts well over five metres (16 feet) readily observable from a guided boat tour on Yellow Water. Smaller lizards include Merton's Water Monitor, a large varanid that nets fish and tadpoles from shallow pools with its tail. There are a number of other beautifully patterned monitors and resident snakes including the Oenpelli Python, unique to Kakadu National Park. This snake is probably Australia's largest and yet it was only discovered in the early 1970s, an indication of how much more Kakadu has to offer. The large Pig-nosed Turtle — one of six known species of freshwater turtle in the park — was discovered in Kakadu in the 1970s. Until then, it was known to exist in New Guinea but was only known in Australia from Aboriginal X-ray paintings in a park rock art 'gallery' at Nourlangie.

The landscapes, too, rich in tropical splendour and brilliant wildflowers, are part of the natural wealth of this national park. Each of the six Aboriginal seasons centred around the 'wet' and the 'dry', produce a shifting scenic

spectacle. Most striking are the grand waterfalls gushing off the escarpment during the wet season or *Gudjewg*, the millions of waterfowl massing on the retreating waters of the dry season or *Gurrung*, and the spectacular electrical storms of the pre-wet season or *Gunumeleng*.

Lands of the Gagudju People

Aboriginal people have been part of the Kakadu (derived from the Aboroginal word *Gagudju*) landscape for at least 62,000 years. Over the generations they have watched the seas come and go across the lowlands. Seventeen clans live here and some still regard the undersea landscape as land endowed with the special and sacred places of the great creation ancestors.

Hundreds of magnificent sandstone galleries along the escarpment and outliers document Aboriginal life over the past 30,000 years in multi-coloured ochres and beeswax. The brilliant rock art includes the enchanting multi-coloured X-ray art and thousands of beautifully rhythmic Mimi paintings in red ochre. Two outstanding galleries – at Ubirr in an East Alligator sandstone outlier and beneath the southern edge of Nourlangie Rock – also reveal elements of Aboriginal life.

At Ubirr, the artsite trail introduces visitors to a long series of symbolic ritual paintings and to a great cavern with its walls decorated with numerous X-ray illustrations of fish and other animals caught nearby – an unbelievable menu. The Nourlangie gallery carries a huge mural of ceremonial figures relating to the dynamic Lightning Dreaming story. Visitors to Nourlangie can also see extraordinarily beautiful images in red, yellow and white ochres of kangaroos and dancing spirit people.

Beginning to Understand Kakadu

Visitors have a wide range of options for enjoying Kakadu, including guided boat tours, 4WD access to wild gorges and waterfalls, recreational fishing, a great variety of walking tracks, guided multi-day bushwalks, camping, guided nature walks, scenic flights, interpreted Aboriginal art galleries and Aboriginal-guided activities.

Considerable park interpretive activity describes the natural and cultural stories of this important World Heritage Area owned and, to a significant degree, managed, by the Aboriginal people. The cultural centre is an essential stop before proceeding into the park.

Top: *In July, after the wet season, the lush green of the Nadab (or Ubirr) floodplain spreads to the horizon from the Ubirr lookout.*

Above: *Occupation sites near this X-ray painting at the Burrungguy artsite, along the south side of Nourlangie Rock, are more than 20,000 years old.*

NITMILUK NATIONAL PARK

Katherine Gorge Splits the Plateau

The dominating feature of Nitmiluk National Park, located 32 kilometres (19.9 miles) from Katherine and 350 kilometres (217 miles) south along the Stuart Highway from Darwin, is the great gorge that slices through the scenic Arnhem Land Plateau. The Katherine River rises to the north-east and zigzags across the plateau following the geometric course of joints and faults in the sandstones. Once across the border of the park, the river channel soon deepens to form the spectacular 30-kilometre (18.6-mile) Katherine Gorge.

In the dry season, the gorge consists of 13 stretches of water separated by rocky bars. During the wet season, from January to March, these bars lie under metres of water and the dense, narrow riverbank vegetation of Weeping Paperbark and *Pandanus* is submerged for weeks.

Around the gorge a vast plateau of hummock grass savanna stretches to the park border and beyond into Arnhem Land. A mix of grasses, shrubs and slender palms grow in the faults dissecting the sandstone, with pockets of monsoon rainforest and plateau swamp surviving in the wetter areas. More than 175 bird species occur in the park, including the threatened Australian Bustard and Hooded Parrot, the Great Bower Bird and the rare Chestnut-quilled Rock Pigeon.

Nitmiluk National Park was established in 1962 and handed back to the Djauan Aboriginal people in 1989. Since then, the 2,921-square-kilometre (1,128-square-

Opposite: *Katherine Gorge traces a series of giant faults or cracks in the ancient sandstone for 30 kilometres (20 miles).*

Above right: *Red-tailed Black Cockatoos,* Calyptorhynchus banksii, *frequently visit Nitmiluk to feed on buds and flowers.*

mile) park has been co-managed by the Djauan and the Northern Territory Parks and Wildlife Commission.

Home of the Freshwater Crocodile

Most visitors come to the park in the winter dry season, when the waters have subsided and the gorge is navigable. Organized cruises upriver leave from the jetty at the mouth of the gorge. The river is slow moving, broad and deep. Once between the great walls, the channel narrows and wildlife such as Azure Kingfishers and Great Egrets are often seen along the water's edge. Fruit bats hang in colonies from flowering Silver-leaf Paperbarks after spending the night feeding on figs.

Wary two-metre (six-foot) Freshwater Crocodiles bask in the sun on exposed rocks, usually near narrow sandbanks where their eggs may be incubating in the warm sand. Few hatchlings survive predation by hungry Mitchells Water Monitors, Sand Monitors, Water and Olive pythons, Barramundi fish, Black-necked Storks and other waders. The park plays a major role in the conservation of these usually harmless crocodiles by protecting their critical nesting habitat.

About three kilometres (almost two miles) upriver, visitors must change barges, walking across the rock bar to the next step up the 'ladder' as the gorge makes one of its right angle bends into another quiet reach kilometres long. Springwater seeps from the base of the gorge wall here and in the mossy mass a number of ferns give cool shady cover for insect-devouring sundews, Tawny Bladderworts and pink Trigger Plants. Up above, *Livistona loriphylla* palms grow in clefts and on ledges, while towards the sunny rim the vivid crimson blossoms of a tree-sized spider flower plant stand out against the glowing walls of hardened sandstone.

Location: 32 km (19.9 miles) east of Katherine, surrounding the Katherine River Gorge, Northern Territory.

Climate: Dry monsoon tropical; summer, maximum temperature 35° C (95° F) with extreme humidity and storms; 950 mm (312 inches) rain almost all through November to March; dry season in winter, with warm to hot clear days and cold nights.

When to go: Most comfortable in the cooler months of April–October, best May–September; wildlife and wildflower viewing best between March and July; waterfalls, March.

Access: By sealed road from Katherine to boat ramp, to track heads at Katherine Gorge entrance and to Edith Falls. By air to nearby Katherine.

Permits: Camping permits available from the national parks office at Katherine. Booking for main park campground advisable.

Equipment: Broad-brimmed hat, light day clothing, strong walking shoes or boots, swimming gear, warm clothes for evening, sunscreen, first-aid kit, insect repellent, daypack, waterbottle.

Facilities: Park camping area with power and full facilities, general store, visitor information centre, ranger guiding service, 10 marked walking tracks from 1.5–76 km (1–47 miles) in length, guided boat tours up the gorge and canoe hire at park, full range of accommodation and vehicle hire at Katherine.

Watching Wildlife: The park offers varied wildlife opportunities from March–July; riverlife is most easily seen from June–October.

Visitor Activities: Guided boat tours, walking, nature study, birdwatching, swimming, single day and overnight canoe trips.

(Map caption) **Nitmiluk National Park** — To Stuart Hwy, Edith Falls, Sweetwater Pool, Darwin, N, Katherine Gorge, Park HQ, To Katherine

Right: *The Great Bower Bird builds its bowers under the cover of low vegetation, living or dead, paving the entrance with white objects.*

Below: *Paddlers spot a Little Pied Cormorant,* Phalacrocorax malanoleu-cos, *while canoeing Katherine Gorge.*

The Thirsty Plateau

The broken surface of the plateau surrounding Katherine Gorge is criss-crossed with joint lines and faults. Trenches and deep gullies separate massive blocks and huge boulders, providing an intricate series of micro-environments. These shelter numerous reptiles from predators in the park, such as the Australian Kestrel and Black Kites.

Hard, spiny Spinifex Grass fills many of the crevasses, even smothering whole boulders. Sand Palms, Turkey Bush and many other colourful shrubs, including several grevilleas, draw in large numbers of honeyeaters during the prolific flowering seasons. Eucalypts, too, produce masses of flowers, attracting a myriad insects as well as Red-collared Lorikeets, Silver-crowned Friarbirds and the large Red-tailed Black Cockatoos. Around the edge of swampy patches, very rare Hooded Parrots make their nests by burrowing into turreted termite mounds.

Exploring the Park

Ten tracks into the Nitmiluk's dry wilderness provide excellent opportunities to discover the park's fauna and the cooler months of June, July and early August are the best times to visit. Early in the morning or late in the afternoon there is a good chance of seeing the large Antilopine Wallaroo, the largest macropod in the area. Much of the wildlife is nocturnal so the four long overnight walks or the canoe trips lasting several days allow visitors to observe the animals when they are at

Left: *The walls of Katherine Gorge, near Butterfly Gorge, glow a golden-pink in the sunlight.*

Below left: *From May to November the Kapok Bush,* Cochlospermum fraseri, *lights up the woodlands and stony slopes of the park.*

Below: *Freshwater Crocodiles,* Crocodylus johnstonii, *lay their eggs in the sandbanks and beaches of the gorge.*

their most active. The Djauan Valley walk offers access to both plateau and gorge wildlife, as well as some fine examples of the park's Aboriginal rock art. When night-spotting for nocturnal wildlife, use a strong torch and try to avoid walking on snakes during the warmer months.

WEST MACDONNELL NATIONAL PARK

Red and Purple Desert Refuge

The West MacDonnell National Park lies across a vast section of the MacDonnell Ranges, stretching for 160 kilometres (99 miles) west of Alice Springs in the heart of arid Australia. This is a tortured land pressured into ranges 300 million years ago, with its most resistant quartzite rocks standing today as high jagged orange and red ridges cut with deep purple-shaded gulches. The Simpson, Hugh, Ellery, Serpentine, Finke, Ormiston and Redbank rivers and creeks have all sliced through the MacDonnells, leaving gaps and gorges with deep, cold, life-giving pools surrounded by vegetation.

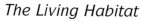

Individual gaps and waterholes were once protected in small reserves. The Northern Territory Conservation Commission acquired some intervening pastoral leases, arranged land transfers and finally, in 1992, the West MacDonnell National Park was born. The park occupies a total of 2,070 square kilometres (799 square miles).

Refuge from the Browning

What has been termed 'the browning of Australia', by Mary White in her remarkable book of the same name, began about 20 million years ago as Australia drifted north into the middle latitudes and on to the tropics. As the drying process continued, forest conditions deteriorated. Forests gradually became woodlands, then dried further to become scrublands, savannas or shrublands.

Opposite: *Ellery Gorge is typical of a number of attractive water gaps cut by rivers across the mountains of the park.*

Above right: *White-trunked Ghost Gums, Eucalyptus papuana, are typical of the MacDonnell Ranges.*

In Australia's centre, these ultimately evolved into the mixed desert communities present today. Changing vegetation meant changing animal habitat. Mountain ranges provided some protected valleys and some extra rainfall and runoff. The deep, cooler gorges held permanent life-giving waterholes and, along with southern mountain aspects like those at Ormiston and Serpentine gorges, became refuges for both vegetation and wildlife.

The Living Habitat

Five significant plant communities are found within the park: outwash woodlands and scrub, as at Simpsons Gap and Ellery Gap; waterholes and wet areas as at Boggy Hole in Finke Gorge; gorges and cliffs, best represented at Ormiston and Redbank gorges; high mountain slopes and mountain tops, as around Mt Giles or Mt Sonder; and the grass and shrublands of the Simpsons Gap area and near the Ochre Pits and Ormiston Pound. The Parks and Wildlife Commission has almost finished linking this mosaic of communities with a 220-kilometre (137-mile) walking track, the Larapinta Trail, from Alice Springs historic telegraph station to Redbank Gorge.

The outwash woodlands are the most biologically productive of the park's ecosystems, irrigated and fertilized each time the rapid runoff from storms sweeps nutrients from the mountain slopes to be dissipated in their deep soils and gravels. The largest Ghost Gums are found in these outwash areas, which are also home to ancient River Red Gums growing by the channels, their many hollows sheltering parrots, bats, geckoes and varanid lizards. Stands of the most spectacular chalky white Ghost Gums, Ironwoods with pendulous bright green leaves, Long-leaved Corkwoods and large Mulga are all to be found near the drive into Simpsons Gap.

Location: Stretching west for 160 km (99 miles) from the Stuart Highway near Alice Springs.

Climate: Summer can be stormy, with an average maximum temperature of 36° C (97° F) and an average minimum of 23° C (73° F); winter is usually clear with some severe frosts, an average maximum temperature of 22° C (72° F) and an average minimum of 7° C (45° F).

When to Go: Most comfortable climate in the cooler months from April–November. Wildflowers best July–September after a wet winter.

Access: By sealed road via Larapinta Drive and Namatjira Drive to Glen Helen from Alice Springs. All side roads to sites are sealed except the road to Redbank Gorge.

Permits: Camping fees should be paid at the national parks office in nearby Alice Springs.

Equipment: Light daytime clothing, warm evening wear, strong shoes or boots, windjacket in winter, sketch pad, swimming gear, first-aid kit; broad-brimmed hat, sunscreen, adequate drinking water.

Facilities: A range of accommodation is available at nearby Alice Springs, campgrounds in the park, toilets and showers at Ormiston. Larapinta Trail multi-day walk; self-guided interpreted walks at Ormiston, Ochre Pits, Simpsons Gap. Sun shelters and picnic areas. Visit Alice Springs Desert Park first.

Watching Wildlife: Easiest spotting in the evening and early morning beside the waterholes and along Ormiston and Ellery creeks; wildlife is usually widespread and difficult to spot after rains.

Visitor Activities: Walking, swimming, wildlife watching, star gazing, day walks around Ormiston Gorge, difficult overnight walk along the Larapinta Trail, cycling along the Simpsons Gap cycleway.

Right: *A River Red Gum,* Eucalyptus camaldulensis, *grows by one of the lower pools near the camping area at Ormiston Gorge.*

Below: *After rain this Mulla Mulla,* Ptilotus sp., *covers large areas of Mulga country throughout Australia's arid heart.*

In the shelter of steep southern slopes and gorges, the cycad *Macrozamia macdonnellii*, and the fig *Ficus platypoda*, are both remnants of earlier wetter and cooler times. The area's most dramatic relict community, however, is the Red Cabbage Tree Palms of Palm Valley, part of nearby Finke Gorge National Park.

Wild About the MacDonnells

The key to wildlife distribution in the interior is the presence of water, food, shelter and special space requirements for breeding. Of these, water supply is most critical. Waterholes, many of which are permanent, are scattered throughout the ranges. The deepest and largest are in the rocky gaps and scoured channel curves. Very mobile species such as Red Kangaroos and Emus travel in off the grassy plains for food or water as the plains dry out; Euros and rock wallabies, while able to withstand many days without water, are forced from their dry rocky habitat to drink periodically from the gorge waterholes. Seed-eating birds such as finches,

Galahs, Pink Cockatoos, Red-tailed Black Cockatoos, Mallee and Mulga parrots and the Spinifex and Bronze-wing pigeons must drink frequently and are therefore usually found within a short distance of water.

Insectivores, such as the Spinifex Hopping Mouse, or carnivores, such as the giant Perentie – the world's second largest lizard – and the Dingo, get much of their water requirements from the body fluids of their prey. They visit waterholes much less regularly and can live out on the plains, on the dry ridges and sand dunes.

Many of the animals of the centre are nocturnal, in order to escape the heat of the day. While they can be difficult to spot in the wild, they are easily visible in the large nocturnal house at the Alice Springs Desert Park, next to the West MacDonnell park entrance.

For the Visitor

Hubs of interest along the ranges are usually tied into the watery gaps, and all are accessible by 2WD cars and short walks. The water in these gaps is generally not fit

Above: *River Red Gums line the sandy bed of Simpsons Creek after it passes through Simpsons Gap.*

Left: *The park's Inland Bearded Dragon,* Pogona vitticeps, *is frequently seen perched on old stumps.*

Below: *At sunset Galahs fly in from the arid plains to the waterholes in the ranges.*

for drinking without being boiled. The visitor should also be aware that many waterholes are over 10 metres (33 feet) deep and can be very cold. Days can be extremely hot (45° + C/113° + F), particularly in summer, and dehydration occurs very rapidly. Always carry adequate drinking water – two litres per hour of walking per person between 10 am and 4 pm. A siesta is a sensible idea.

Numerous Aboriginal artists of the nearby Hermannsburg school – including the famous watercolourist, Albert Namatjira – experienced the same magic mix of form and the opalescent colours changing through the day that captures the heart and spirit.

The story of the importance of artistic expression in Aboriginal culture is well interpreted at the park's Ochre Pits site. A hill consisting of bands of various coloured rocks – reds, yellows, browns and whites – has been carved away by a creek. The exposed bank was a major source of ochre colours for body and rock painting for the west Arrernte and Luritja people. The interpretive track at the site is suitable for people using wheelchairs.

ULURU – KATA TJUTA NATIONAL PARK

World Heritage Area of the Red Centre

The Uluru–Kata Tjuta National Park and World Heritage Area, located 330 kilometres (205 miles) south-west of Alice Springs by air, occupies 1326 square kilometres (511 square miles) on the edge of the Gibson and Great Victoria deserts. Millions of years of erosion have reduced an immense sedimentary range to the park's famous red lumps of rock emerging from the wide expanse of red, sandy plains.

Uluru is a 348-metre (1,141-foot) mind-boggling monolith of bare red-skinned sandstone, measuring 9.4 kilometres (5.8 miles) around its base. Thirty kilometres (18.6 miles) away, Kata Tjuta raises its 36 rounded 'heads' of conglomerate rocks (Kata = heads; Tjuta = many). The largest, Mount Olga, is 546 metres (1,791 feet) high.

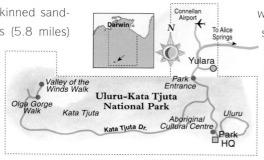

The park was once part of the Petermann Aboriginal Reserve, part of which was established under a Northern Territory Ordinance as a reserve for the 'purpose of a national park' in 1958. In 1977 the Federal Government proclaimed 'Uluru (Ayers Rock–Mount Olga) National Park' within its present boundary and the park also became one of Australia's first UNESCO World Biosphere Reserves. The park was finally handed back to the traditional Anangu Aboriginal owners in 1985 and is now jointly managed by the Aboriginal owners and the federal department, Environment Australia. It received World Heritage listing in 1987 for its natural values and was listed as a cultural landscape in 1994.

Opposite: Uluru (Ayers Rock) is framed by an ancient Desert Oak, Allocasuarina decaisneana, in the foreground.

Above right: Pink Cockatoos, Cacatua leadbeateri, nest in dead Desert Bloodwood tree hollows at the base of Uluru.

Aboriginal Land

According to the Anangu – the local Pijantjatjara owners of the park – the mountains, vegetation, wildlife and people were all formed during the Tjukurpa ('chook-oor-pa'). This is the creation time, which explains the origin of things and gives meaning and order to all aspects of life. Each feature of the landscape is the result of the movements of the creation ancestors, which have been given desert wildlife and plant identities. The sagas of the giant snakes Kuniya the Woma Python and Liru the poisonous King Brown are particularly significant – so much so that the park's magnificent cultural centre, a memorial to the handback, was designed in the shape of two coiled snakes.

People are the custodians of particular stories about place and, as places can't exist without their creation story, people are also an intrinsic part of place – true custodians of the land. For this reason, an interpreted walk around the base of Uluru is the richest experience for the park visitor. Some people take three hours, others take 10, such is the fascination of this beautiful place. One creation story concerns the lazy, sneaky Sleepy Lizard who stole the Bellbird hunters' wounded Emu. A towering grey lichen shape representing smoke and scales shows how Sleepy Lizard was smoked from his sheltering cave high on Uluru's western end.

Red Heart not Dead Heart

Over the decades, many people have died from the intense heat and lack of water in the area, but the Anangu lived a healthy 'bush tucker' life here for thousands of years, collecting and hunting for about four hours each day. The wonderfully shaped surfaces of

Location: 450 km (280 miles) south-west by road from Alice Springs on the edge of the Gibson and Great Victorian deserts.

Climate: Arid interior with a summer average maximum temperature of 37° C (97° F) and average minimum of 22° C (72° F), oppressive with storms; winter has an average maximum of 22° C (72° F) and an average minimum of 7° C (45° F) with clear, sunny days. Annual rain average of 250 mm (9.9 inches). Extreme UV.

When to Go: April–November. Best May–September. Flowers carpet the desert after rain in spring, when birds such as chats arrive and Red Kangaroos begin breeding.

Access: By road along sealed Stuart and Lasseter highways: 450 km (280 miles) from Alice Springs via Erldunda, or 625 km (388 miles) via unsealed Mereenie Loop. By air from State capitals, Broome in Western Australia and Cairns in Queensland.

Permits: Five-day park entry fee from entrance station; no accommodation available in park.

Equipment: Strong non-slip walking shoes, light daytime clothing, warm evening clothes, broad-brimmed hat, sunscreen, waterbottle, sunglasses, fly veil, field guides.

Facilities: Park cultural centre, resort visitor centre and display, walking tracks, Aboriginal guides and rangers, picnic area, sunset and dune viewing areas. Full range of accommodation available at Ayers Rock Resort, Yulara (on perimeter), hire cars, tours, coaches and light aircraft/helicopters for joyflights.

Watching Wildlife: Birds about the mountain edges and waterholes, park has the largest reptile list in Australia, mainly lizards, best seen from March–April and September–November. Flowers after rain.

Visitor Activities: Walking (note: Anangu do not want climbers on Uluru), Aboriginal cultural studies, star gazing, desert natural history.

Above: *After winter rains the desert sands bloom with Annual Yellowtop, pink Paper Daisies and Sturt's Desert Pea.*

Top right: *This Early Nancy, Wurmbea centralis, flowers in August and is only found beside three creeks at Kata Tjuṯa.*

Above right: *The Honey Grevillia, Grevillia eriostachya, is a major source of nectar for birds.*

Uluṟu act as a vast roof, collecting rain when it falls and channelling it into deep rock holes, one of which is the home of Wonampi, the great ancestral serpent that looks after the waters of the desert.

Zebra Finches, Crested Pigeons with wings which whistle, flaming crested Pink Cockatoos, Fairy Martins, Pied Butcherbirds and Australian Kestrels are most commonly seen about the waterholes. There are about 180 bird species on the park list, but many, such as the Crimson Chats and White-faced Herons, are vagrants or migrants, flying in when the rainfall conditions suit them.

In the temporary, shallow rockholes on the top of Uluṟu, Shield Shrimps like tiny Horseshoe Crabs will pass through their whole life cycles in a week or so, finally succumbing to the sun-heated water following a breeding frenzy. Drought will come and, like many desert plants and animals, the tiny eggs will wait in the dust for the next miraculous storm to trigger them into activity.

An Abundance of Plants

Most people have great trouble recognizing the area as desert because it grows over 700 plant species highly adapted to the rigours of the arid environment. About a hundred of these species provide food, water, medicines, cement, fuel and tools. Trees such as Mulga and Ironwood provided extremely hard, edge-holding properties, perfect for spears, digging sticks, throwing sticks and clubs.

Grevilleas and hakeas produce masses of flowers dripping in nectar, which is used to make sweet, high-energy drinks. *Nicotianum* is a source of the stimulant alkaloid nornicotine and used in a plug, or *Mingkaḻpa*, which is tucked under the lower lip. Pituri, a *Duboisia* species, was once thrown into waterholes, the drug it contains seeping into the water, immobilizing the Emus that drank it.

'Pukulpa Pitjama Ananguku Ngurakutu'

'The Aṉangu welcome you to Aboriginal land' is a very genuine welcome to all visitors to Uluṟu. However, visitors often find a national park quite different from the one they expected. Usually their expectations include climbing Uluṟu. On arrival they discover that the route up the Rock is a sacred route that for Aborigines was restricted to critical ceremonial activity. The Aṉangu, too, take the welfare of visitors as a serious responsibility and so when a major accident or death occurs on the Rock, and there have been more than 30 deaths, the community goes into a highly disruptive 'sorry' ceremonial.

Many other restrictions flow from the recognition of the living culture of this place as well as from the dangers inherent in any desert area. It is important to acknowl-

Above: *Sunset paints the domes of Kata Tjuta; Mount Olga is the highest on the right.*

Left: *Thorny Devils, Moloch horridus, are most frequently seen in April and October.*

Far left: *The Mutitjulu waterhole is tucked into the side of Uluru – an oasis for people and wildlife.*

Below left: *Tiku, an Anangu woman, demonstrates the use of the wirra – a wooden tool used for digging Honey Ants and Witchetty Grubs.*

Overleaf: *Uluru at sunset is an unforgettable daily spectacle for hundreds of spellbound visitors.*

edge the cultural and natural universal values of this most significant World Heritage Area and to avoid using Uluru–Kata Tjuta in a careless recreational way.

SUMMARY OF IMPORTANT NATIONAL PARKS

The following is a brief summary of 39 important Australian national parks and conservation parks that are not already described in this book. They have been selected from a list of over 500 such areas established by the States or Territories, or at a Federal level. Together, they cover the major landforms and ecosystems of the continent. There are many other equally significant areas of other denominations that protect habitat and landscapes. When planning a trip to a national park, contact the management authority listed in the 'Useful Addresses', either directly or by mail. Most have brochures.

Federal National Parks

Booderee National Park (63 sq km/24 sq miles). Proclaimed 1992 as Jervis Bay. Wet and dry heath, woodlands and forest; adjoining marine reserve. Returned to Aboriginal ownership and under joint management.

Christmas Island National Park (87 sq km/34 sq miles). In the Indian Ocean. Proclaimed 1980. Limestone and guano on volcanics with rainforest cover. Red Crab migration in November.

Queensland

Bunya Mountains National Park (117 sq km/45 sq miles). Declared 1908. High (1,135m/443ft) ridge on the Great Divide with major stands of Bunya Pines in warm temperate to subtropical rainforest; abundant wildlife and fine walking tracks.

Hinchinbrook Island National Park (399 sq km/154 sq miles). Declared 1932. Dramatic granite mountains, waterfalls, mixed tropical rainforest, rich mangrove forests, range of littoral environments; much in wilderness condition. Dugongs in sheltered Missionary Bay. Famous 2-5 day East Coast Walking Trail accesses this classic park.

Lakefield National Park (5,370 sq km/2,073 sq miles). Declared 1979. Major tropical lowland area; fringing rainforest, open forest, savanna, grasslands, mangrove forest, estuaries, mudflats. Major bird habitats; Black Cockatoo, Jabiru, waders, Golden-shouldered Parrot. Estuarine Crocodile habitat.

Simpson Desert National Park (10,120 sq km/3,906 sq miles). Declared 1967. True desert of parallel dunes, claypans, sandplain and gibber plain covered with spinifex hummock grassland mixed with desert shrubs; little or no water. 4WD access with special equipment only.

Undara Volcanic National Park (615 sq km/237 sq miles). Declared 1993. World's longest lava tubes (caves) in complex volcanic area on a granite base. Collapses are filled with dry rainforest. Rich mammal fauna; many bats.

Whitsunday Islands National Park (170 sq km/65 sq miles). Declared 1944. A group of beautiful mountainous continental islands with fine beaches, estuaries and fringing coral reefs. Part of Great Barrier Reef World Heritage Area.

New South Wales

Barrington Tops National Park (405 sq km/156 sq miles). Declared 1969. Subtropical rainforest, wet open forest, cool temperate rainforest, sub-alpine woodlands and grasslands. Fine walking, wildlife, forest photography and viewing; trout fishing.

Deua (829 sq km/320 sq miles) and **Wadbilliga National Parks** (795 sq km/307sq miles). Contiguous along the south-coast eastern escarpment. Both declared 1979. Dramatic, very steep, forested wilderness ranges; wild river valleys rich in wildlife, particularly kangaroos and wallabies (large macropods). Limestone caves in Deua area. Hard bushwalking country.

Morton National Park (1,627 sq km/628 sq miles). Declared 1934 . Sandstone plateau, 600 m (968 ft) high, with deeply entrenched gorges cut by the tributaries of the Shoalhaven and Kangaroo Rivers. Open forests, warm temperate rainforest, scrubland and heath; fine streams, rich wildlife. Many peripheral walking tracks but mostly wilderness.

Mutawintji National Park (689 sq km/266 sq miles). Declared 1967. Arid low, red sandstone ranges, exquisite valleys and caverns with many Aboriginal art/engraving sites; diverse woodlands with grasslands on extensive northern downs. Many parrots, Euros and kangaroos.

New England National Park (324 sq km/125 sq miles). Declared 1967. On New England escarpment, 1,566 -120 m (5,136 -394ft); ranging from wilderness cool temperate to subtropical rainforest, with tall open forested ridges and valleys. Walking tracks from Point Lookout which has a superlative panorama to the coast.

Sturt National Park (3,106 sq km/1,199 sq miles). Declared 1972. Arid plains, tablelands, mesas and downs; acacia scrublands and grasslands. Red Kangaroos, Emus, raptors, parrots, cockatoos and wrens. Historic settlement remains; wilderness quality.

Warrumbungle National Park (215 sq km/83 sq miles). Declared 1954. Radial ridges and valleys of the old Warrumbungle Volcano 500-1,205m (1,640-3,952ft). Forested; ideal walking and camping; highly photogenic. Koalas, kangaroos and numerous bird species, especially parrots.

Australian Captial Territory

Namadgi National Park (1,058 sq km/408 sq miles). Declared 1980. Northern section of the Australian Alps National Parks, adjacent to Kosciuszko. Wet and dry open forest, eucalypt woodlands, subalpine bogs, grasslands and herb fields.

Victoria

Errinundra National Park (256 sq km/99 sq miles). Declared 1988. Finest remaining stands of warm temperate rainforest in the State with tall wet sclerophyll forest, mostly in a wilderness condition.

Hattah-Kulkyne National Park (480 sq km/185 sq miles). Declared 1960. Murray River overflow lake country bordered by magnificent River Gum forest and mallee-covered dunes to the west and south; large populations of waterbirds and kangaroos. A RAMSAR Convention wetland and World Biosphere Reserve.

Otway National Park (129 sq km/50 sq miles). Declared 1979. The wild gorge of the lower Snowy River is centrepiece. Wilderness forest and rugged ranges with Brushtail Rock Wallabies, Common Wombats, Grey Kangaroos and numerous parrots and cockatoos are featured.

Wyperfield National Park (3,568 sq km/1,377 sq miles). Declared 1909. This park has massive dunes and sandplains covered with mallee and richly flowering heath surround a series of usually dry lakes rich in wildlife including Mallee Fowl; fine springtime walking country.

Tasmania

Ben Lomond National Park (165 sq km/64 sq miles). Declared 1947. Alpine area with fine winter skiing and summer wildflower walks. Dramatic dolerite landscape.

Maria Island National Park (115 sq km/44 sq miles). Declared 1972. A scenic east-coast island with a long settlement history by Aboriginals, convicts, whalers, farmers and miners; all are now gone but their past activities have produced a fascinating network of tracks and mosaic of habitats. Rich wildlife area with Forester Kangaroos and Cape Barren Geese.

Mount William National Park (139 sq km/54 sq miles). Declared 1973. This warm northeastern coastal park has fine beaches, dramatic granite headlands and offshore islets. Its forests, woodlands, heaths and wetlands are rich wildlife and wildflower habitats.

Walls of Jerusalem National Park (518 sq km/200 sq miles). Declared 1981. Glaciated landscape; hundreds of subalpine tarns and lakes; Button Grass plains and ancient cool temperate rainforest habitats; much wildlife. Part of Tasmanian Wilderness World Heritage Area.

South Australia

Belair National Park (8.4 sq km/3 sq miles). Declared 1891. First national park in the State. Adelaide Hills woodland and heathland; noted for wildflowers in spring and historic features.

Coffin Bay National Park (291 sq km/112 sq miles). Declared 1982. A notable coastal wilderness with fine beaches, headlands, cliffs and heathlands. There is abundant oceanic, coastal and heathland wildlife, particularly in spring.

Coorong National Park (467 sq km/180 sq miles). Declared 1966. Very long coastal lagoon behind a massive ocean beach dune barrier at mouth of Murray River. Littoral vegetation running into woodland and mallee. Major wetland bird-nesting area, particularly for pelicans; a RAMSAR site of international importance.

Lake Eyre National Park (13,493 sq km/5,208 sq miles). Declared 1985. Vast wilderness saltlake complex below sea level including eastern dunes, saltpans and Cooper Creek of the Tirari Desert. Fills on rare

occasions and becomes a breeding area for incredible numbers of pelicans, ducks, stilts and others. Major fossil deposits.

Nullarbor National Park (5,883 sq km/2,271 sq miles). Declared 1979. A shrub-covered limestone plateau with a wild cliffed edge that drops to the Great Australian Bight. There are numerous sink holes and vast caverns (Koonalda). This park is noted for clifftop whale-watching and for Southern Hairy-nosed Wombats.

Western Australia

Cape Le Grand National Park (316 sq km/122 sq miles). Declared 1948. Magnificent coastline of grand headlands, beaches, coves, dunes and wetlands. All heath and scrub covered land, ablaze with wildflowers in spring, attracting vast numbers of honey-eating birds. Whale-watching, fishing, walking and swimming are ideal activities.

Stirling Range National Park (1,157 sq km/446 sq miles). Declared 1957. Dramatic and beautiful ranges rise abruptly from the south coastal plain near Albany. A brilliant wildflower area with over 1000 species (60 endemic), including the Kingia and 45 orchid species.

Walpole–Nornalup National Park (159 sq km/61 sq miles). Declared 1972. Two inlets are the core of this coastal park. Fine stands of mighty Karri trees, 90 metres high, and Tingle trees. Abundant wildlife. Extensive visitor developments, particularly the tree-top walk.

Northern Territory

Finke Gorge National Park (459 sq km/177 sq miles). Declared 1967. Long meandering sandstone gorge of great beauty; magnificent gum trees along sandy bed. Relict Palm Valley in a side gorge. 4WD access along river bed. Abundant wildlife.

Gregory National Park (12,882 sq km/4,972 sq miles). Declared 1990. Part of world's largest cattle station on the Victoria River. Very diverse monsoon tropical landscape, quartzite gorges, large rivers and lagoons, karst areas and downs, Boab trees, savanna and woodland. Boat, car and 4WD access. Estuarine Crocodiles.

Gurig National Park (2,265 sq km/874 sq miles). Declared 1981. Aboriginal-owned park on a low hilly peninsular with deeply indented shoreline. Rich protected tropical marine area, monsoon forest, palm forest and savanna with major wetlands and prolific wildlife, including Estuarine Crocodiles. A historic area.

Keep River National Park (572 sq km/221 sq miles). Declared 1981. Monsoon woodlands and savanna; beautiful red sandstone gorge. Caverns with very fine Aboriginal paintings.

Litchfield National Park (1,458 sq km/563 sq miles). Declared 1986. Waterfalls, deep sandy plunge pools, lagoons, rock features and idyllic monsoon rainforest and woodlands near Darwin. Abundant wildlife; Agile Wallabies, Rainbow Pittas, Imperial Pigeons.

Watarrka National Park (1,057sq km/408 sq miles). Declared 1989. Magnificent Kings Canyon and rare desert hummocky sandstone plateau landscape; deep waterholes, desert wildflowers, raptors, galahs, Ghost Gums and Desert Oaks. Walking tracks.

USEFUL ADDRESSES

Australian Conservation Foundation
340 Gore Street, Fitzroy VIC 3065

Department of Conservation & Land
50 Hayman Road, Como WA 6152
tel: 08-93340333; fax: (08) 9334 0498;
www.calm.wa.gov.au

Department of Natural Environment & Resources, Outdoor Information Centre
240–250 Victoria Parade
East Melbourne VIC 3002
tel: 03-94124795; fax: 03-92992425

Environment ACT
PO Box 1119, Tuggeranong ACT 2901
tel: 02-62079777; fax: (02) 6207 2227;
http://www.act.gov.au/environ

Environment Australia
GPO Box 636, Canberra ACT 2601
tel: 02-62741111;
http://www.environment.gov.au

Great Barrier Reef Marine Park Authority
2–68 Flinders Street, PO Box 1379
Townsville, QLD 4810
tel: 07-47500700; www.gbrmpa.gov.au

National Parks and Wildlife Service
77 Grenfell Street, Adelaide SA 5001
Tel: 08-82041910; fax: 08-82041919;
www.denr.sa.gov.au

**National Parks & Wildlife Service/
Department of Environment & Land**
134 Macquarie Street, Hobart TAS 7000
tel: 03-62338011; www.parks.tas.gov.au

National Parks & Wildlife Service
PO Box 1967, Hurstville NSW 2220
tel: 02-95856444; fax: 02-95856455;
http://www.npws.nsw.gov.au.

National Parks and Wildlife Service
GPO Box 150; Brisbane QLD 4002
tel: 07-32277801; fax: 07-32277676
www.env.qld.gov.au

Northern Territory Tourist Commission
GPO Box 2532, Alice Springs NT 0871
tel: 1800621336; fax: 1800808666;
www.nttc.com.au

NSW Travel Centre
GPO Box 11, Sydney, NSW. 2000
tel: 132077; fax: 02-9224 4411

Parks Victoria
378 Cotham Road, Kew VIC 3101
tel: 03-94124795;
www.nre.vic.gov.au

Queensland Government Travel Centre
196 Adelaide Street, Brisbane QLD 4000
tel: 131801; www.qtte.com.au

**Queensland National Parks
Information Centre**
Ground Floor, 160 Ann Street
Brisbane QLD 4000

Tasmanian Vistor Information Network
Elizabeth and Davey Streets
Hobart TAS 7001
tel: 03-62308233; www.tourism.tas.gov.au

Territory Parks and Wildlife Commission
PO Box 496, Palmerston NT 0831
tel: 08-89994533; fax: 08-89323849;
www.nt.gov.au

Tourism South Australia
1 King William Street, Adelaide SA 5000
tel: 08-83032033 or 1800882092;
www.tourism.sa.gov.au

Tourism Victoria
Vistor Information Centre, Town Hall
Melbourne VIC 3000
tel: 132842; www.tourism.vic.gov.au

Uluru and Kakadu National Parks
GPO Box 1260, Darwin NT 0800
tel: 08-89464300; fax: 08-89813497

Western Australian Tourist Centre
(GPO Box W 2081)
469 Wellington Street, Perth WA 6000
tel: 1300361351; www.wa.gov.au/gov/watc

Wet Tropics Management Authority
PO Box 2050, Cairns QLD 4870
tel: 07-40520555

World Wide Fund for Nature Australia
GPO Box 528, Sydney NSW 2001
tel: 1800251573

FURTHER READING

Australian Alps Committee (1998) *Explore the Australian Alps.* New Holland, Sydney.

Boland, D.J., *et al* (1984) *Forest Trees of Australia.* Nelson & CSIRO, Melbourne.

Brock, J. (1988) *Native Plants of Northern Australia.* New Holland Publishers, Sydney.

Caruana, W. (1989) *Aboriginal Art.* Thames and Hudson, London.

Church, F. ed., (1999) *Explore Australia.* Viking, Ringwood.

Cogger, H.G. (2000) *Reptiles and Amphibians of Australia.* Reed/New Holland, Sydney.

Costin, A.B., *et al* (1979) *Kosciusko Alpine Flora.* Collins-CSIRO.

Cronin, L. (1994) *Key Guide to Australia's National Parks.* New Holland, Sydney.

Cresswell, I.D. & Thomas, G.M. (1997) *Terrestrial and Marine Protected Areas in Australia.* Environment Australia, Biodiversity Group, Canberra.

Cunningham, G.M., *et al* (1981) *Plants of Western New South Wales.* Government Printer, Sydney.

Fox, A.M. (1983) *Of Birds and Billabongs.* Rigby, Adelaide.

Fox, A.M. (1984) *Australia's Wilderness Experience.* Rigby, Adelaide.

Fox, A.M. (1991) *Centenary Field Guide of Major Parks and Reserves of South Australia.* Government Printer, Adelaide.

Fox, A.M. (1993) *Wilderness.* Steve Parish, Brisbane.

Fox, A.M. (1997) *Guidebook, Mungo National Park.* Beaten Track Press, Canberra.

Fox, A.M. (1997) *Photographing Uluru.* Beaten Track Press, Canberra.

Fox, AM. (1998) *Amazing Facts About Australian Landscapes.* Steve Parish, Brisbane.

Greig, D. (1999) *Field Guide to Australian Wildflowers.* New Holland, Sydney.

Heritage Commission of Australia. (1981) *The Heritage of Australia.* Macmillan, Melbourne.

Hermes, N. (1997) *Explore Wilderness Australia,* New Holland, Sydney.

Neidgie, W., *et al* (1985) *Kakadu Man – Bill Neidgie.* Mybrood, Queanbeyan.

Pizzey, G. & Knight, F. (1998) *Field Guide to the Birds of Australia,* HarperCollins, Sydney.

Shine, R. (1998) *Australian Snakes – A Natural History.* New Holland, Sydney.

Simpson, K. & Day, N. (1993) *Field Guide to the birds of Australia.* Viking, Ringwood.

Strahan, R. (1998) The *Mammals of Australia.* New Holland, Sydney.

Swadling, M. (1995) *Paradise on Earth – The Natural World Heritage List.* IUCN-Harper-MacRae, Columbus.

Talbot, F. ed., (1984) *The Great Barrier Reef.* Readers Digest, Sydney.

Tucker, M. (1989) *Whales and Whale Watching in Australia.* ANPWS, Canberra.

Underhill, D. (1989) *The Australian Wildlife Year.* Readers Digest, Sydney.

Underhill, D. (1993) *Australia's Dangerous Creatures.* Readers Digest, Sydney.

Urban, A. (1990) *Wildflowers and Plants of Central Australia.* Southbank, Melbourne.

White, M. (1986) *The Greening of Gondwana – The Browning of Australia.* Kangaroo Press, Sydney.

Wrigley, J.W. & Fagg, M. (1997) *Australian Native Plants.* Reed Sydney.

Zborowski, P. & Storey, R. (1997) *A Field Guide to Insects of Australia.* New Holland, Sydney.

Photographic Credits

INDEX

Page numbers in **bold** type refer to illustrations.